Miniature Pinscher

By Charlotte Schwartz

lumina
MEDIA

Photographs by Mary Bloom, Isabelle Français, Carol Ann Johnson and Michael Trafford with additional photos by Norvia Behling, T. J. Calhoun, Doskocil, Bill Jonas, Mikki Pet Products and Alice van Kempen.

The publisher wishes to thank the owners of the dogs featured in this book. Also, thanks to Janette Relyea, DVM.

Illustrations by Renée Low and Patricia Peters.

Original Print ISBN 978-1-59378-301-3

This book has been published with the intent to provide accurate and authoritative information in regard to the subject matter within. While every precaution has been taken in the preparation of this book, the author and publisher expressly disclaim any responsibility for any errors, omissions, or adverse effects arising from the use or application of the information contained herein. The techniques and suggestions are used at the reader's discretion and are not to be considered a substitute for veterinary care. If you suspect a medical problem, consult your veterinarian.

lumina MEDIA

2030 Main Street, Suite 1400
Irvine, CA 92614
www.facebook.com/luminamediabooks
www.luminamedia.com

My Miniature Pinscher

PUT YOUR PUPPY'S FIRST PICTURE HERE

Dog's Name _____

Date _____ Photographer _____

Head: In correct proportion to the body. Tapering, narrow with well fitted but not too prominent foreface.

Ears: Set high, standing erect from base to tip. May be cropped or uncropped.

Skull: Appears flat, tapering forward toward the muzzle.

Neck: Proportioned to head and body, slightly arched, gracefully curved, blending into shoulders, muscular.

Eyes: Full, slightly oval, clear, bright and dark even to a true black, including eye rims, with the exception of chocolates.

Muzzle: Strong rather than fine and delicate, and in proportion to the head.

Nose: Black only, with the exception of chocolates.

Lips and Cheeks: Small, taut and closely adherent to each other.

Teeth: Meet in a scissors bite.

Forechest: Well developed.

Color: Solid clear red. Stag red. Black with sharply defined rust-red markings. Chocolate with rust-red markings.

Forequarters: Shoulders clean and sloping with moderate angulation. Elbows close to the body. Legs— As viewed from the front, straight and upstanding. Pasterns strong, perpendicular.

Physical Characteristics of the Miniature Pinscher

(from the American Kennel Club breed standard)

Topline: Back level or slightly sloping toward the rear.

Body: Compact, slightly wedge-shaped, muscular.

Tail: Set high, held erect, docked in proportion to size of dog.

Hindquarters: As viewed from the rear, the legs are straight and parallel. From the side, well angulated. Thighs well muscled. Stifles well defined. Hocks short, set well apart.

Coat: Smooth, hard and short, straight and lustrous, closely adhering to and uniformly covering the body.

Size: 10 inches to 12.5 inches in height allowed, with desired height 11 inches to 11.5 inches measured at highest point of the shoulder blades.

Feet: Small, catlike, toes strong, well arched and closely knit with deep pads. Nails thick, blunt.

Contents

Training Your Miniature Pinscher   85

Be informed about the importance of training your Miniature Pinscher from the basics of housebreaking and understanding the development of a young dog to executing obedience commands (sit, stay, down, etc.).

Health Care of Your Miniature Pinscher   113

Discover how to select a qualified vet and care for your dog at all stages of life. Topics include vaccinations, skin problems, dealing with external and internal parasites and common medical and behavioral conditions.

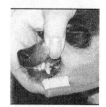

Your Senior Miniature Pinscher   143

Consider the care of your senior Miniature Pinscher, including the proper diet for a senior. Recognize the signs of an aging dog, both behavioral and medical; implement a special-care program with your vet and become comfortable with making the final decisions and arrangements for your senior Miniature Pinscher.

Showing Your Miniature Pinscher   150

Enter the dog show world to find out how dog shows work and how a champion is made. Go beyond the conformation ring to obedience trials and agility trials, etc.

Index   156

Although primarily a companion dog today, the Miniature Pinscher originated as a farm dog in Germany in the 1700s.

MINIATURE PINSCHER

MEET THE "MIN PIN"

It's a narrow dirt footpath beside a country road. Bordering the walkway is a tall row of hedges that separates pedestrians from the private property on the other side. Strolling down the path, you hear dogs barking behind the hedgerow. There are two dogs, small by the sound of their voices, but very determined in their warning alarm. "Keep away" is the loud and clear message.

You come to the corner and follow the footpath around the corner. The hedgerow now opens up to a lovely front yard with a gate and a flower-covered fence. You look beyond the front gate and see the source of the unrelenting barking: two Miniature Pinschers, one dark red and the other black-and-tan. They stand side-by-side, their Toy-dog bodies pulled up to present a fearless image, larger than the dogs themselves, as they warn you to stay off their property. Their proud and alert countenances make you forget their diminutive size.

Suddenly, amid the barking and displaying, the owner emerges from the house beyond

Similar in appearance to the great German guard dog, the Doberman Pinscher, the Miniature Pinscher did not originate from the Doberman and is actually the more ancient of the two breeds.

ior turns from that of fearless guard dogs to that of happy house pets, clowning around at their owner's feet. "This is Bromley," says the owner, pointing to the black-and-tan dog. "She's named after the town where she was born. And my handsome red devil here is Midas. He's the leader of the pack."

A brief neighborly chat later, you bid the lady and her dogs farewell and continue your walk. As you stroll along the country road, you think about Bromley and Midas. You admire their obvious and complete sense of self. You also like the love and respect they show their owner. Finally, you like the way they look. You start to suspect that the "Min Pin," as the breed is affectionately called, might be the perfect breed of dog for you, too. You've been contemplating buying a dog for some time. Now, considering your lifestyle, the Miniature Pinscher appears to be just what you've been seeking in a companion.

the front yard. She speaks softly yet firmly to them. "Quiet! Enough!" The dogs look back at her and comply as they run to greet her. She bends down to praise them and then moves forward again. The dogs give one final bark as if to say, "We'll have the last word here!" Again they race back to the gate.

As you chat with the dogs' owner, you watch as their behav-

Doing your homework and researching the breed now becomes a priority. You are anxious to learn more about this plucky little dog who thinks he's a giant. Maybe, before long, you'll have a Min Pin in your own home!

ORIGIN OF THE BREED

The Miniature Pinscher originated on German farms in the 1700s.

They were bred to be ratters and were probably developed by crossing Dachshunds and Italian Greyhounds, with the addition of some terrier blood. Contrary to common belief, the Miniature Pinscher does not originate from the Doberman Pinscher, a large look-alike breed that did not evolve until a century later. In fact, the only similarity between Dobermans and Min Pins is the fact that they both claim terriers among their ancestors.

Originally, the Miniature Pinscher was called the Reh Pinscher, a name that referred to a small red deer that roamed the German forests. Until the late 1800s, the breed was produced without much regard to standardization. As long as the dog was small and could be an effective rat hunter, it was acceptable as a Reh Pinscher.

In 1895, the Pinscher Klub, now known as the Pinscher Schnauzer Klub, emerged as the inspiration for the breed. Standards of perfection were set, correct temperament was spelled out in detail and colors were defined clearly. This marked the formal beginning of this unique little breed. It was at this time that the official classification of Toy dog was designated. Today, Min Pins are often referred to as the "King of Toys."

Naturally erect ears were a must for the breed in Germany, whereas in America cropped ears were (and still are) permitted as well. Docked tails were called for and coats were to be short and smooth, and were to lie close to the skin. Coat colors were defined as red, stag red (red mingled with

CROPPED EARS
In the United States, the Miniature Pinscher's ears may be cropped or natural, but must stand erect. Cropped ears, shown here, are prohibited in Australia and Africa as well as in the UK. Cropping Miniature Pinscher ears in Great Britain was outlawed at the beginning of the 20th century.

WHAT IS EAR CROPPING?

Ear cropping consists of surgically trimming the ear leathers and then training the ears to stand upright. Originally, cropping was done to prevent the ears from being bitten by any adversary. With fighting dogs and terriers, cropped ears gave the opponent less to hang on to. Ear cropping also was considered important for cosmetic purposes, as it gives the dog a very smart look. Today the tradition of cropping ears has been banned in some countries; in these countries, dogs of any breed with cropped ears cannot be shown. Dogs can be shown in the United States with either cropped or uncropped ears, but certain breeds are rarely seen in the ring with uncropped ears. Erect ears are a must in the Miniature Pinscher; in the US, they can be either cropped or natural.

black hairs), black and rust or chocolate and rust.

The Min Pin was defined as a proud, vigorous little dog with a hackneyed gait and a fearless presence. He must be alert and graceful, with an unshakable devotion to his master. In addition, he must display speed and courage. In other words, he's a dog with an attitude and he lets the whole world know it!

These standards of perfection have changed little from those early days. They remain the guiding blueprints for the breed around the world.

FROM SCANDINAVIA TO THE REST OF THE WORLD

The breed's first appearance beyond its land of origin was in the Scandinavian countries. Even today it is a favorite breed in Denmark. From that region, it spread throughout Europe (it is still a favorite today in the Netherlands and Italy) and into the British Isles, where people embraced its vibrant personality and great intelligence, as well as its ease of care.

From 1905 to the beginning of World War I, the Miniature Pinscher grew rapidly in popularity as more and more people became aware of the breed's desirable characteristics. During the war, however, breeding and the refinement of breed traits came to a halt. Then, in about 1915, interest in the breed renewed and serious breeding resumed.

Shortly thereafter, German immigrants brought Miniature Pinschers with them to the United States. It is thought that the breed first arrived here around 1919, with the first representative of the breed being registered with the American Kennel Club (AKC) in 1925. The breed was first shown in the AKC's Miscellaneous Class, although numbers in the early years were small. At that time, the breed was registered as the Pinscher (Toy).

Then, in 1929, the Miniature Pinscher Club of America was formed with the aim of getting the breed officially recognized in the Toy Group. The breed first was moved to the Terrier Group and shown there, but by 1930 the club had achieved its goal and the breed earned classification as a member of the Toy Group, with the name Pinscher (Miniature). It kept this name until 1972, when it was changed to Miniature Pinscher, the name by which we know these dogs today.

The breed's popularity continued to grow well into the 20th century and, by 1998, the Miniature Pinscher in the United States ranked 16th in AKC registrations, which was a great improvement over the ranking of 53rd in popularity 20 years earlier. The breed began the 21st century in the AKC's top 20, with registrations around the 20,000 mark. As a matter of fact, one of the greatest American Toy dogs of all time was the red Miniature Pinscher named Ch. Rebel Roc's Casanova von Kurt.

The Miniature Pinscher Club of America (MPCA) has overseen the breed standard and the revisions it underwent in the 20th century. The first standard was established in 1929, and it has evolved into the standard currently in effect, last revised in 1980. Interestingly, some early versions of the standard, being based on German standards of the time, made reference to the Min Pin's appearing similar in looks to the Doberman! Obviously those references were deleted, and no

GENUS CANIS

Dogs and wolves are members of the genus *Canis*. Wolves are known scientifically as *Canis lupus* while dogs are known as *Canis domesticus*. Dogs and wolves are known to interbreed. The term "canine" derives from the Latin-derived word *Canis*. The term "dog" has no scientific basis but has been used for thousands of years. The origin of the word "dog" has never been authoritatively ascertained.

BRAIN AND BRAWN
Since dogs have been inbred for centuries, their physical and mental characteristics are constantly being changed to suit man's desires for hunting, retrieving, scenting, guarding and warming their masters' laps. During the past 150 years, dogs have been judged according to physical characteristics as well as functional abilities. Few breeds can boast a genuine balance between physique, working ability and temperament.

Min Pins are popular as show dogs in the US and around the world. In the ring, they display an impressive presence that belies their small stature.

mention of the Doberman has appeared in the Miniature Pinscher standard since 1950.

Aside from developing the breed standard, the MPCA has safeguarded the best interests of the breed in all aspects since the Min Pin's early years in the US, and the club continues as the breed's parent club today. Some of its functions are to regulate breeding, conduct health research and education, coordinate breed rescue and assist prospective owners in making a wise decision about choosing the breed. It also organizes shows and events for the Miniature Pinscher; the club's annual specialty is a major event in the dog world for Min Pins and their devotees. The club publishes also publishes a timely and informative newsletter, the *Pinscher Patter.*

It is interesting to note that there are far fewer ancient artistic records of the Miniature Pinscher than there are of many other breeds. This fact is easily understood when you consider that Min Pins were dogs of the farmers, not of the aristocracy. Hunting hounds and giant-breed guard dogs as well as the tiny Toy dogs bred to accompany "milady" were recorded often in artwork. However, through the years, some Miniature Pinschers have been depictedby artists in oil and watercolors, in carvings and engravings and on tapestries used

Gregarious and intelligent, the Min Pin requires an owner who is available and willing to accept the responsibility (and affection) of this "King of Toys."

as wall and floor coverings.

For example, in 1856, the artist George Earl painted an oil portrait of a white English terrier named Prince. Studying that image, one can appreciate the striking resemblance, except for the color, between Prince and the modern-day Miniature Pinscher, even to the cropped ears. Of course, the written word also serves as documentation for the Miniature Pinscher's historical significance.

MINIATURE PINSCHER

The Miniature Pinscher is not a simple breed. For example, there are two basic questions one might ask about any dog: Do they bark much and are they aggressive toward people or other dogs?

With many breeds, these questions would be answered simply with either yes or no. Not so with the Miniature Pinscher! The answer to both of these questions is both yes *and* no; thus, an explanation is necessary. There are many facets of the Min Pin's character, and the best way to get to know the whole dog is to define each aspect individually. We will first become more acquainted with the Miniature Pinscher before attempting to answer these questions.

PHYSICAL CHARACTERISTICS

We begin our study of the breed with an overall impression of the physical traits of the dog. What does he look like? The Min Pin is small, compact, muscular and alert. Weighing in between 6 and 8 lb (3–4 kg), he should stand between 10 and 12.5 inches at the shoulder. He is well balanced, with a short, close coat and an elegance of style that gives him an abundance of eye-appeal.

He is self-possessed, fearless and high-spirited, which is visibly evident in his well-groomed, proud countenance. He is a dog that, despite the onset of old age, continues to be energetic and playful throughout his life.

The overall look of a Min Pin is that of a sturdy little dog without an extra inch of coat or useless trimmings. The dog's elegance results from a solidly built body, a gracefully curved neck, a head that tapers from the top of the skull to the dark-tipped nose and ears that sit high on the head above slightly oval, dark eyes.

PERSONALITY

The Miniature Pinscher is an intelligent dog, quick to learn whatever his master wants to teach him. A major asset of the breed is his eagerness to please master and family. He believes he owns his home and the people in it. Though he can be stubborn at times, he loves the limelight and will clown around endlessly for a crowd who shows its enthusiasm

The picture of balance and symmetry, the Min Pin is a small, compact, attentive dog with all aspects in proportion.

with applause. In addition, the Min Pin has a charming sense of humor.

Min Pins do well in the sports of agility and obedience competition, and also trick training. With their many talents, they make stylish show dogs.

The Min Pin is an adaptable dog, readily adjusting to a variety of different environments and living situations. He can conform to life in small quarters, such as apartments and small houses, just as well as he can fit into large homes or farms. It is also possible to house-train him to newspaper indoors, making him an ideal pet for those unable to exercise their dogs outdoors.

The Min Pin is a curious dog and, without proper supervision, can get into all sorts of trouble. If he somehow finds his way out of the fenced yard, he will play "catch me if you can!" with his owner for hours. The owner's

The curious Min Pin is always up for something new. This dog enjoys a splash in the kiddie pool.

natural instinct to chase the dog only serves to further incite the dog's desire to play! This can be a dangerous situation for the dog, which is why a securely fenced yard and supervision are always necessary, and the dog should always be kept on lead in unfenced areas. A securely fenced-in yard that has been screened carefully for potentially dangerous objects such as nails, broken glass, small tools, hazardous plants, etc., is the ideal way to give the Min Pin all the exercise he needs. However, the owner must be diligent in keeping the area secure by watching out for holes, broken boards and small openings that would allow the dog to escape. You can bet that if the fence has a fault, the dog will find it!

The Min Pin's inquisitiveness can lead him into danger zones inside the home as well. Small objects on tables and countertops are invitations for him to grab them and see what they're all about. Stealing cushions from the couch and pulling out the stuffing is a hazardous activity, to say nothing of the cost of replacing the damaged cushions.

Chewing on electrical cords and tearing apart objects that might contain poisonous substances can prove fatal, so great care must be taken to create a dog-proof environment and supervise the dog at all times. In the event that an owner cannot keep a watchful eye on his Min Pin, the dog should be contained safely in his own crate.

Since Miniature Pinschers are high-energy dogs, they need to be mentally and physically challenged in order for them to stay in optimum condition. Training the Min Pin is a given. Many people feel that small dogs don't need schooling, but this is a serious misconception. Little dogs are cute, but they do naughty things just as big dogs do. However, adorable little dogs are usually more easily forgiven! This line of reasoning is a recipe for trouble with a dog. If a Miniature Pinscher does something he shouldn't do, the owner should teach the dog not to repeat the behavior. If the dog gets away with misbehaving, you can be sure that he will do it again and again.

Using physical force to stop the dog from doing something will prove very destructive to the dog/owner relationship. Instead of correcting a bad behavior with negative reinforcement, it is far more effective to reward acceptable behavior right from the beginning. Enrolling in a beginner's obedience course teaches the owner how to train his dog and teaches the headstrong little Min Pin how to pay attention and obey his owner. Thus, dog and owner will build a bond together

DOGS, DOGS, GOOD FOR YOUR HEART!

People usually purchase dogs for companionship, but studies show that dogs can help to improve their owners' health and level of activity, as well as lower a human's risk of coronary heart disease. Without even realizing it, when a person puts time into exercising, grooming and feeding a dog, he also puts more time into his own personal health care. Dog owners establish more routine schedules for their dogs to follow, which can have positive effects on their own health. Dogs also teach us patience, offer unconditional love and provide the joy of having a furry friend to pet!

that will last a lifetime and make living together a rewarding and harmonious experience. Then, instead of living with a cute dog, the owner will live with a cute, well-mannered dog! That's an enviable combination that's hard to beat.

ANSWERING THE QUESTIONS

DOES THE MIN PIN BARK MUCH?
Now, back to the two questions that were posed at the beginning of the chapter. First, does the Miniature Pinscher bark a lot? True to his nickname, the "King of Toys," the Min Pin is fearless and, despite his small size, makes an excellent alarm dog as well as an imposing guardian of home and family. However, his high-pitched, incessant barking can become a nuisance unless he is trained to stop barking on command. When the dog barks unnecessarily or for too long, the owner should speak in a stern voice and say "No! Quiet!" When the dog stops, even if it is only for a moment, the owner should say "Good boy. Good quiet" in a soft, pleasant tone of voice.

If verbal correction proves ineffective, the owner can try using water in a spray bottle. When the dog barks, the owner goes to the dog, says "No! Quiet!" and squirts several sprays of water in the dog's face. Dogs do not like water in their faces, so he will gasp and shake his head. Most importantly, he will stop barking as he shakes his head. At that moment, the owner should begin praising the quiet dog with a soft tone of voice to show approval of the dog's compliance. Generally, a few incidents of using a spray bottle when the dog refuses to quiet down will prove successful. In the future, all you will have to do is show the bottle to the dog to remind him to stop barking on command. Eventually, the simple command of "No! Quiet!" will suffice on its own.

Left untrained, Min Pins can be rowdy, noisy little dogs who bark at the slightest disturbances. When trained, they are well-mannered, quiet dogs who bark only for alarm and cease barking upon command. So the answer to this question is, indeed, both yes and no. Remember Bromley and Midas? It's the owner's choice and a simple matter of training. Setting lifestyle rules should be done when the dog is first acquired. Min Pins are intelligent and, when taught properly, they will accept their leaders and obey the rules because they want to please.

ARE MIN PINS AGGRESSIVE?
Second, are Miniature Pinschers aggressive toward people or other dogs? Again, the answer could be either yes or no; the dog's behavior depends upon the dog's

Many enthusiasts find it difficult to resist the urge to "collect" Min Pins. Breeders can attest to the many affable characteristics of their favorite Toy dog.

THERAPY DOG

When trained properly, Miniature Pinschers make wonderful therapy dogs. They can be taken to schools, hospitals, retirement homes and nursing facilities to cheer up the people there. Because they are small, they can sit on beds or on the laps of elderly people. They also provide unconditional solace and comfort to the sick or lonely; their attention is non-judgmental and always welcomed.

owner. For example, if an owner allows his Miniature Pinscher to bark and run to snap at a visitor's ankles, the dog will think that this behavior is acceptable and will continue to act in this manner whenever someone comes to visit. Before long, the dog will be labeled as vicious and uncontrollable.

As soon as the dog is acquired, the owner should introduce the dog to friends and visitors with a happy tone of voice and gentle petting. When the doorbell rings, the owner can begin the process of conditioning the dog to greet visitors by showing his own pleasure at the prospect of the arrival of guests. The owner's happy tone of anticipation plus a favorite treat for the dog will teach the dog that guests represent good things plus positive attention. Making the association of pleasant events with the arrival of guests helps the dog to learn right from the beginning that people should not be feared or threatened.

Meeting people outdoors or in public places should produce the same kind of pleasure for the dog. The owner can carry a few biscuits in his pocket to give to people who wish to acknowledge the dog with petting and a treat.

In summary, Min Pins can be nuisance barkers if they are not taught properly. In addition, they can be aggressive and nasty if allowed to threaten people or other dogs. Teaching them to be well mannered, friendly and quiet is easy when the dog is young. Changing the bad habits of older, mature dogs is difficult at best. With the right training, they can learn to control themselves, but the owner needs to exercise patience, diligence, consistency and an effective, humane training method. Thus, seeking professional help for correcting the undesirable habits of an older dog is highly recommended.

THINGS TO CONSIDER
Keeping the dog's environment safe, by providing either constant supervision or a safe haven (crate) for times when the owner cannot be with the dog, becomes a permanent necessity when owning a Miniature Pinscher. Regardless of age, they remain curious, quick and fearless. Pet-proofing the home and yard are essential.

Leaving the front door open is an invitation for the Min Pin to race out of the house and beyond. A Min Pin is so quick that the owner rarely sees the dog pass before him as the dog heads for the great outdoors. Consequently, care must be taken to secure the dog whenever a door is opened.

Min Pins think that they are the kings of all they survey. "Fence-fighting" with neighboring dogs is common, so Min Pins

need to be supervised when exercising in the yard. They seem to have no concept of their small size and will boldly threaten larger dogs who come near their property or cross their paths when out for walks. Here again, training for good manners and self-control is a must, just to keep the Min Pin safe from the retaliation of bigger dogs.

Due to the Min Pin's intelligence, he easily can be taught a variety of behaviors to coincide with his owner's lifestyle. For example, Min Pins love to run with the joggers in the family.

Min Pins who are raised with children will willingly accept the children as companions. All children must be properly instructed in how to handle a Toy dog, so that no harm comes to the dog or the child.

Providing the jogger sets a reasonable pace, the Min Pin loves the opportunity to exercise and to interact with a family member.

The Min Pin also can be taught to accept children in his life, providing the children are taught to respect animals. This means teaching children how to handle a dog. Min Pins (or any dog, for that matter) do not like to be yanked and pushed about; rather, they respond well to gentle stroking, petting and soft voices. Miniature Pinschers that are raised with children from puppyhood freely devote themselves to the youngsters. Adult Min Pins who have no previous experience with little ones are usually reluctant to befriend them, and may often show dislike for children. Therefore, care must be taken to supervise the dogs whenever children are present.

Similarly, Min Pins can live peacefully with other pets, providing they are introduced to them during puppyhood. However, supervision is again necessary when a Min Pin lives with a larger dog, simply because his diminutive size puts him at risk for injury during rough play.

Even though the Min Pin is a high-energy dog breed, he loves nothing better than to curl up on a sofa or bed with his owner for a cuddle. He also takes readily to travel and loves to ride in the car. He should be taught to ride in the

car in his crate, as this is the safest way for dogs to travel. He can be accustomed to this on short trips, and eventually will come to accept the crate as his own space in the car.

Ideally, the Miniature Pinscher owner should be a person who has the time and energy to devote to training the dog. The desire for a loyal, attentive companion, combined with the interest in channeling the dog's abundant energy and the ability to understand and accept the breed's challenging characteristics, is necessary if one is to become a successful Min Pin owner.

HEALTH CONCERNS IN THE MINIATURE PINSCHER

Generally speaking, Min Pins are healthy and long-lived, often living to 12 to 14 years of age. Unlike many dog breeds, they are not plagued by a multitude of health problems. However, there are a few health concerns that exist within the breed, and every prospective owner should be aware of these.

LEGG-CALVE-PERTHES DISEASE

This is a problem of the hip joint that is caused by a lack of blood supply to the femoral head. Onset usually occurs before one year of age, and usually one leg is affected. Limping and obvious pain when the leg is extended

Miniature Pinschers welcome affection from and quiet time with their owners, along with exercise and socialization on a regular basis to balance their high-energy personalities.

are two easily recognized symptoms. Treatment involves surgically removing the femoral head. Alternatively, restricted exercise and cortisone treatments can sometimes prove effective.

PATELLAR LUXATION

This is a dislocation of the kneecap that results from an injury or a congenital deformity. It can occur either in one or in both legs. Severe pain and limping occur in most cases. Treatment ranges from rest and no physical exercise to surgical procedures to reconstructing the affected joint.

MANGE, COLOR MUTATIONS AND OTHER SKIN PROBLEMS

These problems are often linked together. Demodectic mange can be localized or generalized. Mange requires the application of ointment to small areas of

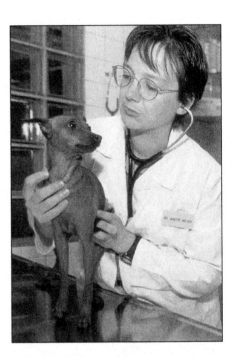

affected skin or, if the entire body is affected, total body bath dips. Demodectic mange occurs when large numbers of micro-scopic parasitic mites inhabit the

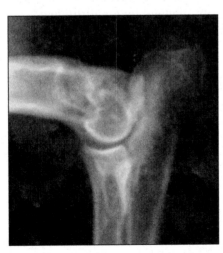

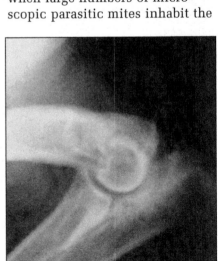

hair follicles and skin of normal dogs. In some cases, the dogs acquire the mites from their dams shortly after birth. In older dogs, demodectic mange may signal cancer or another serious internal disease.

Color mutations in Min Pins are caused by abnormal hair follicles with dilute coat colors, such as blue-gray or fawn. Both the hair and the skin are affected, causing color mutant alopecia, a genetic disease that causes hair loss, which can lead to secondary skin infections. There is no known cure for alopecia.

Veterinary experts advise Min Pin breeders not to breed for the mutant blue coat color. The blue color is a dilution of the black coat color and a result of a defect in coat color genes.

These hair and skin problems are often life-long. Abnormal hair follicles in dogs with mutant coat colors can cause abnormal oil secretions. This, in turn, predisposes the dog to secondary skin infections, which can and do last a lifetime.

Epilepsy

Epilepsy is quite a common problem in dogs. It is the result of a malfunction in the electrical impulses transmitted by the brain to the nerve cells. Excessive discharge of those impulses can cause sudden seizures or convulsions. There is no cure for epilepsy, but it can be controlled with daily medication. Dogs with controlled epilepsy live full, productive lives. Many have obtained breed and obedience titles as well as awards in tracking, agility and other areas of the dog sport. Generally speaking, once the proper medication is found for the individual dog, the animal's personality and temperament will not change.

Progressive Retinal Atrophy (PRA)

This eye problem has been seen in the Miniature Pinscher. PRA is hereditary and causes blindness, and there is no cure. The retina (the light-sensitive membrane at the back of the eyeball) degenerates, thus causing blindness. However, a veterinary ophthalmologist can test puppies for potential PRA and provide the breeder with a certificate of satisfaction, which can be passed on to the new owners. A potential owner should always ask the breeder for verification of his pup's freedom from eye anomalies.

Other Health Issues

Deafness and kidney stones have occasionally been seen in the Miniature Pinscher. However, the incidents have occurred in such small numbers that these conditions are not considered breed-specific problems.

MINIATURE PINSCHER

At the very first glance, the Miniature Pinscher appears to be a well-balanced dog. He does not possess anything in excess; rather, all parts of his body combine to create a graceful, agile and compact animal that is instantly appealing to the eye.

This Min Pin look and type are maintained at all times by conscientious breeders who follow what is called the "breed standard." This standard presents in words the definition of perfection for the Miniature Pinscher. The standard is what is used by dog show judges to create for themselves a mental picture of the perfect Miniature Pinscher.

National kennel clubs and individual breed clubs create and monitor these standards for each breed registered with the national kennel clubs. Each standard includes the ideal specifications for temperament, body structure, gait and type for a given breed. In other words, breed standards spell out the details of the perfect representative of each breed.

The American Kennel Club (AKC) standard begins with a description of the Miniature Pinscher's general appearance. It goes on to cover details regarding the dog's physical characteristics, temperament and movement. It also defines the disqualifying features that make the dog ineligible to be shown in conformation competition.

Without this set of specifications, the breed soon would begin to deviate in its features to such a

MEETING THE IDEAL

The American Kennel Club defines a standard as: "A description of the ideal dog of each recognized breed, to serve as an ideal against which dogs are judged at shows." This "blueprint" is drawn up by the breed's recognized parent club, approved by a majority of its membership, and then submitted to the AKC for approval. The AKC states that "An understanding of any breed must begin with its standard. This applies to all dogs, not just those intended for showing." The picture that the standard draws of the dog's type, gait, temperament and structure is the guiding image used by breeders as they plan their programs.

There is no such thing as a "perfect" dog of any breed. In conformation competitions, the dogs are judged using the standard as the basis for comparison to see which comes closest to the ideal.

degree that, sooner or later, it would no longer be recognizable as a Miniature Pinscher. The standard then becomes the guideline that breeders follow in order to produce, and continue to produce, quality dogs that are typical of the breed.

THE AKC STANDARD FOR THE MINIATURE PINSCHER

General Appearance: The Miniature Pinscher is structurally a well balanced, sturdy, compact, short-coupled, smooth-coated dog. He naturally is well groomed, proud, vigorous and alert. Characteristic traits are his hackney-like action, fearless animation, complete self-possession, and his spirited presence.

Size, Proportion, Substance: Size—10 inches to 12.5 inches in height allowed, with desired height 11 inches to 11.5 inches measured at highest point of the shoulder blades. Disqualification—Under 10 inches or over 12.5 inches in height.

Length of males equals height at withers. Females may be slightly longer.

Head: In correct proportion to the body. Tapering, narrow with well fitted but not too prominent foreface which balances with the skull. No indication of coarseness. Eyes full, slightly oval, clear, bright and dark even to a true black, including eye rims, with the exception of chocolates, whose eye rims should be self-

HACKNEY GAIT
The AKC standard calls for the Min Pin to have a "hackney-like" gait. A hackney gait is defined as a high lifting of the front feet, like that of a hackney horse.

colored. Ears set high, standing erect from base to tip. May be cropped or uncropped. Skull appears flat, tapering forward toward the muzzle. Muzzle strong rather than fine and delicate, and in proportion to the head as a whole. Head well balanced with only a slight drop to the muzzle, which is parallel to the top of the skull. Nose black only, with the exception of chocolates which should have a self-colored nose. Lips and cheeks small, taut and closely adherent to each other. Teeth meet in a scissors bite.

Neck, Topline, Body: Neck proportioned to head and body, slightly arched, gracefully curved, blending into shoulders, muscular and free from suggestion of dewlap or throatiness. Topline—Back level or slightly sloping toward the rear both when standing and gaiting. Body compact, slightly wedge-shaped, muscular. Forechest well developed. Well-sprung ribs. Depth of brisket, the base line of which is level with points of the elbows. Belly moderately tucked up to denote grace of structural form. Short and strong in loin. Croup level with topline. Tail set high, held erect, docked in proportion to size of dog.

Forequarters: Shoulders clean and sloping with moderate angulation coordinated to permit the hackney-like action. Elbows close to the body. Legs—Strong bone development and small clean joints. As viewed from the front, straight and upstanding. Pasterns strong, perpendicular. Dewclaws should be removed. Feet small, catlike, toes strong, well arched and closely knit with deep pads. Nails thick, blunt.

Hindquarters: Well muscled quarters set wide enough apart to fit into a properly balanced body. As viewed from the rear, the legs are straight and parallel. From the side, well angulated. Thighs well muscled. Stifles well defined. Hocks short, set well apart. Dewclaws should be removed. Feet small, catlike, toes strong, well arched and closely knit with deep pads. Nails thick, blunt.

Coat: Smooth, hard and short, straight and lustrous, closely adhering to and uniformly covering the body.

Color: Solid clear red. Stag red (red with intermingling of black hairs). Black with sharply defined rust-red markings on cheeks, lips, lower jaw, throat, twin spots above eyes and chest, lower half of forelegs, inside of hind legs and vent region, lower portion of hocks and feet. Black pencil stripes on toes. Chocolate with rust-red markings the same as specified for blacks, except brown pencil stripes on toes. In the solid red and stag red a rich vibrant medium to dark shade is preferred. Disqualifications—Any color other than listed. Thumb mark (patch of black hair surrounded by rust on the front of the foreleg between the foot and the wrist; on chocolates, the patch is chocolate hair). White on any part of dog which exceeds one-half inch in its longest dimension.

Gait: The forelegs and hind legs move parallel, with feet turning neither in nor out. The hackney-like action is a high-stepping, reaching, free and easy gait in which the front leg moves straight forward and in front of the body and the foot bends at the wrist. The dog drives smoothly and strongly from the rear. The head and tail are carried high.

Temperament: Fearless animation, complete self-possession, and spirited presence.

Disqualifications:
- Under 10 inches or over 12.5 inches in height.
- Any color other than listed.
- Thumb mark (patch of black hair surrounded by rust on the front of the foreleg between the foot and the wrist; on chocolates, the patch is chocolate hair).
- White on any part of dog which exceeds one-half inch in its longest dimension.

Approved July 8, 1980
Reformatted February 21, 1990

The ears are set on high and the eyes are clear, dark and bright with a slightly oval shape.

Profile of a quality example of the Miniature Pinscher.

Faults: Ewe neck; straight shoulders; weak topline; shallow chest; weak pasterns; flat feet; general lack of substance.

Faults: Short, thick neck; bullish front and shoulders; heavy body; low-set tail; straight in rear.

Correct hackney gait, showing high lifting of the front legs and head held proudly.

Incorrect gait.

Profile of proper head with natural erect ears.

Profile of proper head with cropped ears.

Correct forequarters with well-developed chest and strong, straight legs.

Weak forequarters with narrow chest and legs turning out.

MINIATURE PINSCHER

PUPPY APPEARANCE
Your puppy should have a well-fed appearance but not a distended abdomen, which may indicate worms or incorrect feeding, or both. The body should be firm, with a solid feel. The skin of the abdomen should be pale pink and clean, without signs of scratching or rash. Check the hind legs to make certain that dewclaws were removed, as breeders have this done when the pups are a few days old.

From casual observations and some research, you've almost reached the final decision that the Miniature Pinscher is the breed of dog you want. Min Pins are long-lived, so owning one will be a long-term commitment. Now on to the next step.

You've located a breeder who has a litter of Min Pin puppies. You meet the puppies, two males and a female, and begin chatting with the breeder. Here are some questions you need to ask yourself and/or the breeder in order to determine whether buying one of these puppies is the best option for you.

1. Is the place where the pups are kept clean? Is the area free of unpleasant odor? Do the puppies have adequate space in which to play, eat, sleep and relieve themselves?
2. Are the puppies anxious to meet you and friendly toward you and the breeder? A puppy that runs away from people and/or cowers in a corner is too shy. He may even grow up to be a fear-biter.

3. Have you met one or both of the puppies' parents? Are they friendly, clean and healthy-looking? Puppies learn a lot from their parents; an aggressive parent may teach the puppy to act that way, too.

4. What type of food do the pups eat and how much/how often are they fed? Ask the breeder about the puppies' diet and how to continue feeding. If possible, observe their stool to make sure it is well-formed and solid. A loose stool can indicate worms, infection or bacterial infestations, all of which require the attention of a vet and indicate that the pups may have some sort of health problem.

5. Do the puppies have bright, clear eyes and sweet-smelling breath? Are their coats clean and shiny? Are their noses cool? A healthy puppy will have all of these traits, plus he will be free of parasites and have no signs of a cough. Always check the bite of your selected puppy to be sure that it is neither overshot nor undershot. This may not be too noticeable on a young puppy, but will become more evident as the pup gets older.

6. Do I want a male or a female puppy? Your initial research into the breed should have pointed out the basic differences between male and

ARE YOU PREPARED?
Unfortunately, when a puppy is bought by someone who does not take into consideration the time and attention that dog ownership requires, it is the puppy who suffers when he is either abandoned or placed in a shelter by a frustrated owner. So all of the "homework" you do in preparation for your pup's arrival will benefit you both. The more informed you are, the more you will know what to expect and the better equipped you will be to handle the ups and downs of raising a puppy. Hopefully, everyone in the household is willing to do his part in raising and caring for the pup. The anticipation of owning a dog often brings a lot of promises from excited family members: "I will walk him every day," "I will feed him," "I will house-train him," etc., but these things take time and effort, and promises can easily be forgotten once the novelty of the new pet has worn off.

female Min Pins, such as the fact that males should be neutered and females should be spayed. Males can develop the bad habit of lifting their legs indoors unless they are trained to relieve themselves outdoors only. Males may also have an urge to wander; therefore, again, training and constant supervision are necessary. While it is necessary to train and supervise all dogs, females are usually more home-oriented and less likely to wander. Do these sex-related traits affect your choice of a male or a female Min Pin?

7. What is the puppies' genetic history? The breeder should be eager to explain this to you.

A wire pen, called an "ex-pen," is used to safely confine the litter and give them a taste of the great outdoors.

PEDIGREE VS. REGISTRATION CERTIFICATE

Too often new owners are confused between these two important documents. Your puppy's pedigree, essentially a family tree, is a written record of a dog's genealogy of three generations or more. The pedigree will show you the names as well as performance titles of all dogs in your pup's background. Your breeder must provide you with a registration application, with his part properly filled out. You must complete the application and send it to the AKC with the proper fee. Every puppy must come from a litter that has been AKC-registered by the breeder, born in the USA and from a sire and dam that are also registered with the AKC.

The seller must provide you with complete records to identify the puppy. The AKC requires that the seller provide the buyer with the following: breed; sex, color and markings; date of birth; litter number (when available); names and registration numbers of the parents; breeder's name; and date sold or delivered.

He should be happy to give you the name and address of his vet as a reference. The vet can verify the parents' good health.

The breeder will supply the necessary documentation along with your chosen puppy. These include any medical certificates, registration documents and the pedigree, which traces your puppy's family tree. Full instructions on feeding and caring for the puppy should also be included to make the pup's transition from the breeder's home to your home as easy as possible for all concerned.

FINDING A BREEDER AND PUPPY

You may be wondering how to find Miniature Pinscher breeders. Locating a litter of Miniature Pinschers should not present a problem for the new owner. You should inquire about breeders who enjoy good reputations in the breed. You are looking for an established breeder with outstanding dog ethics and a strong commitment to the breed. New owners should have as many questions as they have

Min Pins do best in homes with polite older children who understand how to handle small dogs with care.

TEMPERAMENT COUNTS

Your selection of a good puppy can be determined by your needs. A show potential or a good pet? It is your choice. Every puppy, however, should be of good temperament. Although show-quality puppies are bred and raised with emphasis on physical conformation, responsible breeders strive for equally good temperament. Do not buy from a breeder who concentrates solely on physical beauty at the expense of personality.

doubts. An established breeder is indeed the one to answer your four million questions and make you comfortable with your choice of the Miniature Pinscher. An established breeder will sell you a puppy at a fair price if, and only if, the breeder determines that you are a suitable, worthy owner of his dogs. An established breeder can be relied upon for advice, no matter what time of day or night. A reputable breeder will accept a puppy

PUPPY PERSONALITY

When a litter becomes available to you, choosing a pup out of all those adorable faces will not be an easy task! Sound temperament is of utmost importance, but each pup has its own personality and some may be better suited to you than others. A feisty, independent pup will do well in a home with older children and adults, while quiet, shy puppies will thrive in homes with minimal noise and distractions. Your breeder knows the pups best and should be able to guide you in the right direction.

back, without questions, should you decide that this is not the right dog for you.

When choosing a breeder, reputation is much more important than convenience of location. Do not be overly impressed by breeders who run brag advertisements in the dog presses about their stupendous champions. The real quality breeders are quiet and unassuming. You hear about them at dog shows and trials, by word of mouth. You may be well advised to avoid the novice who lives only a few miles away. The local novice breeder, trying so hard to get rid of that first litter of puppies, is more than accommodating and anxious to sell you one. That breeder will charge you as much as any established breeder. The novice breeder isn't going to interrogate you and your family about your intentions with the puppy, the environment and training you can provide, etc. That breeder will be nowhere to be found when your poorly bred, badly adjusted four-pawed monster starts to growl and spit up at midnight or eat the family cat!

While health considerations in the Miniature Pinscher are not nearly as daunting as in most other breeds, socialization is a breeder concern of immense importance. Since the Miniature Pinscher's temperament can vary from line to line, socialization is the first and best way to encourage a proper, stable personality.

Choosing a breeder is an important first step in dog ownership. Fortunately, the majority of Miniature Pinscher breeders is devoted to the breed and its well-being. New owners should have no problem finding a reputable breeder who doesn't live on the other side of the country. The American Kennel Club and the Miniature Pinscher Club of America are able to refer you to breeders of quality Miniature Pinschers in your region. Potential owners are encouraged to attend dog shows (or trials) to see the Miniature Pinschers in action, to meet the owners and handlers firsthand and to get an idea of what Miniature Pinschers look like outside a photographer's lens. Provided you approach the handlers when they are not busy with the dogs, most are more than willing to answer questions, recommend breeders and give advice.

Once you have contacted and met a breeder or two and made your choice about which breeder is best suited to your needs, it's time to visit the litter. Keep in mind that many top breeders have waiting lists. Sometimes new owners have to wait a year or more for a puppy. If you are really committed to the breeder

"YOU BETTER SHOP AROUND!"

Finding a reputable breeder who sells healthy pups is very important, but make sure that the breeder you choose is not only someone you respect but also someone with whom you feel comfortable. Your breeder will be a resource long after you buy your puppy, and you must be able to call with reasonable questions without being made to feel like a pest! If you don't connect on a personal level, investigate some other breeders before making a final decision.

If the breeder from whom you are buying a puppy asks you a lot of personal questions, do not be insulted. Such a breeder wants to be sure that you will be a fit provider for his puppy.

whom you've selected, then you will wait (and hope for an early arrival!). If not, you may have to continue your search and choose

INHERIT THE MIND
In order to know whether or not a puppy will fit into your lifestyle, you need to assess his personality. A good way to do this is to interact with his parents. Your pup inherits not only his appearance but also his personality and temperament from the sire and dam. If the parents are fearful or overly aggressive, these same traits may likely show up in your puppy.

another breeder. Don't be too anxious, however. If the breeder doesn't have a waiting list, there is probably a good reason. It's no different than visiting a restaurant with no clientele. The better restaurants always have waiting lists—and it's usually worth the wait! Besides, isn't a puppy more important than a fancy dinner?

Since you are likely to be choosing a Miniature Pinscher as a pet and not a show dog, you simply should select a pup that is friendly and attractive. Miniature Pinschers generally have small litters, averaging five puppies, so selection is limited once you have located a desirable litter. While the basic structure of the breed has little variation, temperament may present trouble in certain strains. Beware of the shy or overly aggressive puppy; be especially conscious of the nervous Miniature Pinscher pup, and don't let sentiment or emotion trap you into buying the runt of the litter.

Breeders commonly allow visitors to see the litter by around the fifth or sixth week, and puppies leave for their new homes between the tenth and twelfth week. Breeders who permit their puppies to leave early are more interested in a profit than their puppies' well-being. Puppies need to learn the rules of the pack from their dams, and most dams continue teaching the pups manners and dos and don'ts until they leave for new homes. Breeders spend significant amounts of time with the Miniature Pinscher toddlers so that they are able to interact with the "other species," i.e., humans. Given the long history that dogs and humans have, bonding between the two species is natural but must be nurtured. A well-bred, well-socialized Miniature Pinscher pup wants nothing more than to be near you and please you.

COMMITMENT OF OWNERSHIP

After considering all of these factors, you have most likely made some very important decisions about selecting your puppy. You have chosen the Miniature Pinscher, which means that you have decided which characteristics you want in a dog and what type of dog will best fit into your family and lifestyle. If you have selected a breeder, you have gone a step further—you have done your research and found a responsible, conscientious person who breeds quality Miniature Pinschers and who should be a reliable source of help as you and your puppy adjust to life together. If you have observed a litter in action, you have obtained a firsthand look at the dynamics of a puppy "pack"

TIME TO GO HOME
Breeders rarely release puppies until they are eight to ten weeks of age. This is an acceptable age for most breeds of dog, excepting Toy breeds, like the Min Pin, which are not released until around 10 to 12 weeks, given their petite sizes. If a breeder has a puppy that is 12 weeks of age or older, he is likely well socialized and house-trained. Be sure that he is otherwise healthy before deciding to take him home.

and, thus, you should have learned about each pup's individual personality—perhaps you have even found one that particularly appeals to you.

However, even if you have not yet found the Miniature Pinscher puppy of your dreams, observing pups will help you learn to recognize certain behavior and to determine what a pup's behavior indicates about his temperament. You will be able to pick out which pups are the leaders, which ones are less outgoing, which ones are confident, which ones are shy, playful, friendly, aggressive, etc. Equally as important, you will learn to recognize what a healthy pup should look and act like. All of these things will help you in your search, and when you find

YOUR SCHEDULE . . .
If you lead an erratic, unpredictable life, with daily or weekly changes in your work requirements, consider the problems of owning a puppy. The new puppy has to be fed regularly, socialized (loved, petted, handled, introduced to other people) and, most importantly, allowed to visit outdoors for toilet training. As the dog gets older, it can be more tolerant of deviations in his feeding and toilet relief.

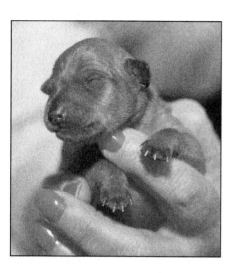

the Miniature Pinscher that was meant for you, you will know it!

Researching your breed, selecting a responsible breeder and observing as many pups as possible are all important steps on the way to dog ownership. It may seem like a lot of effort...and you have not even taken the pup home yet! Remember, though, you cannot be too careful when it comes to deciding on the type of dog you want and finding out about your prospective pup's background. Buying a puppy is not—or *should* not be—just another whimsical purchase. This is one instance in which you actually do get to choose your own family! You may be thinking that buying a puppy should be fun— it should not be so serious and so much work. Keep in mind that your puppy is not a cuddly stuffed doll or decorative lawn ornament, but a living creature that will become a real member of your family. You will come to realize that, while buying a puppy is a pleasurable and exciting endeavor, it is not something to be taken lightly. Relax...the fun will start when the pup comes home!

Always keep in mind that a puppy is nothing more than a baby in a furry disguise...a baby who is virtually helpless in a human world and who trusts his owner for fulfillment of his basic needs for survival. In addition to food, water and shelter, your pup needs care, protection, guidance and love. If you are not prepared to commit to this, then you are not prepared to own a dog.

"Wait a minute," you say. "How hard could this be? All of my neighbors own dogs and they seem to be doing just fine. Why should I have to worry about all

A newborn Min Pin puppy is tiny and fragile. The breeder puts so much time into raising and caring for these babies, and he wants to ensure that this care continues when the pups are ready to go to new homes.

The leaders of the litter will be obvious as you watch the pups play together and roughhouse with each other.

QUALITY FOOD
The cost of food must be mentioned. All dogs need a good-quality food with an adequate supply of protein to develop their bones and muscles properly. Most dogs are not picky eaters but, unless fed properly, can quickly succumb to skin problems.

of this?" Well, you should not worry about it; in fact, you will probably find that once your Miniature Pinscher pup gets used to his new home, he will fall into his place in the family quite naturally. But it never hurts to emphasize the commitment of dog ownership. With some time and patience, it is really not too difficult to raise a curious and exuberant Miniature Pinscher pup to be a well-adjusted and well-mannered adult dog—a dog that could be your most loyal friend.

PREPARING PUPPY'S PLACE IN YOUR HOME
Researching your breed and finding a breeder are only two aspects of the "homework" you will have to do before taking your Miniature Pinscher puppy home. You will also have to prepare your home and family for the new addition. Much as you would prepare a nursery for a newborn baby, you will need to designate a place in your home that will be the puppy's own. How you prepare your home will depend on how much freedom the dog will be allowed. Whatever you decide, you must ensure that he has a place that he can "call his own."

When you bring your new puppy into your home, you are bringing him into what will become his home as well. Obviously, you did not buy a puppy so that he could take control of your house, but in order for a puppy to grow into a stable, well-adjusted dog, he has to feel comfortable in his surroundings. Remember, he is leaving the warmth and security of his mother and littermates, as well as the familiarity of the only place he has ever known, so it is important to make his tran-

CRATE-TRAINING TIPS

During crate training, you can partition off the section of the crate in which the pup stays. If he is given too big an area, this will hinder your training efforts. Crate training is based on the fact that a dog does not like to soil his sleeping quarters, so it is ineffective to keep a pup in an area that is so big that he can eliminate in one end and get far enough away from it to sleep. Also, you want to make the crate den-like for the pup. Blankets and a favorite toy will make the crate cozy for the small pup; as he grows, you may want to evict some of his "room-mates" to make more room. It will take some coaxing at first, but be patient. Given some time to get used to it, your pup will adapt to his new home-within-a-home quite nicely.

sition as easy as possible. By preparing a place in your home for the puppy, you are making him feel as welcome as possible in a strange new place. It should not take him long to get used to it, but the sudden shock of being transplanted is somewhat trau-matic for a young pup. Imagine how a small child would feel in the same situation—that is how your puppy must be feeling. It is up to you to reassure him and to let him know, "Little fellow, you are going to like it here!"

WHAT YOU SHOULD BUY

CRATE

To someone unfamiliar with the use of crates in dog training, it may seem like punishment to shut a dog in a crate, but this is not the case at all. In fact, teaching the puppy to enjoy his crate is easy and comes naturally to the dog. More and more breeders and trainers around the world are recommending crates as preferred tools for pet puppies as well as show puppies.

Crates are not cruel—crates have many humane and highly effective uses in dog care and training. Crating the puppy when you can't be there to supervise him will protect the puppy from harm and your home from destruction. A crate is an ideal method for toilet-training the puppy, a crate can keep your dog safe during travel and, perhaps most importantly, a crate provides your dog with a place of his own in your home. It

In addition to a crate, your Min Pin should be provided with a soft dog bed, placed in a central location in the home, so that he begins to feel like a member of your pack.

Your local pet shop should have a wide variety of crates to show you. A small crate should suffice for the Min Pin both as a puppy and at full size.

PHOTO COURTESY OF DOSKOCIL

As far as purchasing a crate, the type that you buy is up to you. It will most likely be one of the two most popular types: wire or fiberglass. There are advantages and disadvantages to each type. For example, a wire crate is more open, allowing the air to flow through and affording the dog a view of what is going on around him while a fiberglass crate is sturdier. Both can double as travel crates, providing protection for the dog in the car. The size of the crate is another thing to consider. Puppies do not stay puppies forever—in fact, sometimes it seems as if they grow right before your eyes. Fortunately, a Min Pin is a small breed, and a small crate should suffice for both a Min Pin pup and fully-grown adult.

BEDDING

A soft pad in the dog's crate will help him feel more at home, and you may also like to give him a small blanket in the crate. These will take the place of the leaves,

serves as a "doggie bedroom" of sorts—your Miniature Pinscher can curl up in his crate when he wants to sleep or when he just needs a break. Many dogs sleep in their crates overnight. With soft bedding and his favorite toy, a crate becomes a cozy pseudo-den for your dog. Like his ancestors, he too will seek out the comfort and retreat of a den— you just happen to be providing him with something a little more luxurious than what his early ancestors enjoyed.

IN DUE TIME

It will take at least two weeks for your puppy to become accustomed to his new surroundings. Give him lots of love, attention, handling, frequent opportunities to relieve himself, a diet he likes to eat and a place he can call his own.

twigs, etc., that the pup would use in the wild to make a den; the pup can make his own "burrow" in the crate. Although your pup is far removed from his den-making ancestors, the denning instinct is still a part of his genetic makeup. Second, until you take your pup home, he has been sleeping amid the warmth of his mother and litter-mates, and while a blanket is not the same as a warm, breathing body, it still provides heat and something with which to snuggle. You will want to wash your pup's bedding frequently in case he has a potty accident in his crate, and replace or remove any bedding that becomes ragged and starts to fall apart.

Toys

Toys are a must for dogs of all ages, especially for curious playful pups. Puppies are the "children" of the dog world, and what child does not love toys? Chew toys provide enjoyment for both dog and owner—your dog will enjoy playing with his favorite toys, while you will enjoy the fact that they distract him from your expensive shoes and leather sofa. Puppies love to chew; in fact, chewing is a physical need for pups as they are teething, and everything looks appetizing! The full range of your possessions—from old dishrag to Oriental carpet—are fair game in the eyes

PLAY'S THE THING

Teaching your Min Pin to play with his toys in running and fetching games is an ideal way to help him develop muscle, learn motor skills and bond with you, his owner and master. He also needs to learn how to inhibit his bite reflex and never to use his teeth on people, forbidden objects and other animals in play. A stern "No bite!" command as you hold his muzzle shut will usually prove effective after several repetitions. Whenever you play with your Min Pin, you make the rules. This becomes an important message to your dog in teaching him that you are the pack leader and control everything he does in life. Once your dog accepts you as his leader, your relationship with him will be cemented for life.

TOYS, TOYS, TOYS!

With a big variety of dog toys available, and so many that look like they would be a lot of fun for a dog, be careful in your selection. It is amazing what a set of puppy teeth can do to an innocent-looking toy, so, obviously, safety is a major consideration. Be sure to choose the most durable products that you can find. Hard nylon bones and toys are a safe bet, and many of them are offered in different scents and flavors that will be sure to capture your dog's attention. It is always fun to play a game of fetch with your dog, and there are balls and flying discs that are specially made to withstand dog teeth.

Play is vital for puppies and adults alike. Provide an array of safe chew toys for your Min Pin and he will amuse himself for hours on end.

of a teething pup. Puppies are not all that discerning when it comes to finding something to literally "sink their teeth into"—everything tastes great!

Miniature Pinscher puppies are fairly aggressive chewers and

only the strongest toys should be offered to them. Breeders advise owners to resist stuffed toys, because they can become de-stuffed in no time. The overly excited pup may ingest the stuffing, which is neither nutritious nor digestible. Similarly, squeaky toys are quite popular, but must be avoided for the Miniature Pinscher. Perhaps a squeaky toy can be used as an aid in training, but not for free play. If a pup "disembowels" one of these, the small plastic squeaker inside can be dangerous if swallowed. Monitor the condition of all your pup's toys carefully and get rid of any that have been chewed to the point of becoming potentially dangerous.

Be careful of natural bones, which have a tendency to splinter into sharp, dangerous pieces. Also be careful of rawhide, which can turn into pieces that are easy to swallow and become a mushy mess on your carpet.

LEAD

A nylon lead is probably the best option, as it is the most resistant to puppy teeth should your pup take a liking to chewing on his lead. Of course, this is a habit that should be nipped in the bud, but, if your pup likes to chew on his lead, he has a very slim chance of being able to chew through the strong nylon. Nylon leads are also lightweight, which is good for a young Miniature Pinscher who is just getting used to the idea of walking on a lead. Be sure to have your pup's lead securely attached to his collar before taking him outdoors. Lively, curious puppies can dart off in seconds and usually run much faster than their owners; the collar and lead will keep your puppy safe and under control. For everyday walking and safety purposes, the nylon lead is a good choice.

As your pup grows up and gets used to walking on the lead, and can do it politely, you may want to purchase a flexible lead. These leads allow you to extend the length to give the dog a broader area to explore or to shorten the length to keep the dog near you.

COLLAR

Your pup should get used to wearing a collar all the time since you will want to attach his ID tags to it. Plus, you have to attach the lead to something! A lightweight nylon collar is a good choice; make sure that it fits snugly enough so that the pup cannot wriggle out of it, but is loose enough so that it will not be uncomfortably tight around the pup's neck. You should be able to fit a finger between the pup and the collar. It may take some time for your

MENTAL AND DENTAL
Toys not only help your puppy get the physical and mental stimulation he needs but also provide a great way to keep his teeth clean. Hard rubber or nylon toys, especially those constructed with grooves, are designed to scrape away plaque, preventing bad breath and gum infection. Puppies will enjoy soft toys during teething, although it is important to supervise your pup with potentially destructible toys.

pup to get used to wearing the collar, but soon he will not even notice that it is there.

FOOD AND WATER BOWLS

You'll need suitable bowls made of ceramic, stainless steel or heavy plastic, one bowl for food and one for water. You may want two sets of bowls, one for inside and one for outside, depending on where the dog will be fed and where he will be spending time. Plastic bowls are more chewable, but dogs tend not to chew on the steel variety, which can be sterilized. It is important to buy sturdy bowls since anything is in danger of being chewed by puppy teeth and you do not want your dog to be constantly chewing apart his bowl (for his safety and for your wallet!).

Make sure that the sides of the bowls are low, since Min Pins are so small. Also, never leave an empty bowl or partially finished food out on the floor, as it can attract ants and other insects. Water always should be cool, fresh and clean.

CLEANING SUPPLIES

Until a pup is house-trained, you will be doing a lot of cleaning. "Accidents" will occur, which is acceptable in the beginning because the puppy does not know any better. All you can do is be prepared to clean up any

FINANCIAL RESPONSIBILITY

Grooming tools, collars, leashes, a crate, a dog bed and, of course, toys will be expenses to you when you first obtain your pup, and the cost will continue throughout your dog's lifetime. If your puppy damages or destroys your possessions (as most puppies surely will!) or something belonging to a neighbor, you can calculate additional expense. There is also flea and pest control, which every dog owner faces more than once. You must be able to handle the financial responsibility of owning a dog.

accidents. Old rags, towels, newspapers and a safe disinfectant are good to have on hand.

BEYOND THE BASICS

The items previously discussed are the bare necessities. You will find out what else you need as you go along—grooming supplies, flea/tick protection, baby gates to partition a room, etc. These things will vary depending on your situation, but it is important that you have everything you need to feed and make your Miniature Pinscher comfortable in his first few days at home.

Pet shops usually stock a wide assortment of leads. Min Pin puppies only need the lightest of nylon leads.

CHOOSE AN APPROPRIATE COLLAR

The BUCKLE COLLAR is the standard collar used for everyday purpose. Be sure that you adjust the buckle on growing puppies. Check it every day. It can become too tight overnight! These collars can be made of leather or nylon. Attach your dog's identification tags to this collar.

The HALTER is for a trained dog that has to be restrained to prevent running away, chasing a cat and the like. Considered the most humane of all restraints, it is frequently used on smaller dogs on which collars are not comfortable.

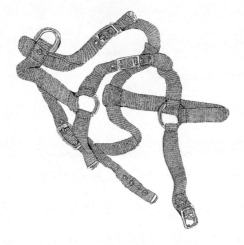

The CHOKE COLLAR is designed for use during training, although it is *not* suitable for use on a Toy dog. It is constructed of highly polished steel so that it slides easily through the stainless steel loop. The idea is that the dog controls the pressure around his neck and he will stop pulling if the collar becomes uncomfortable. *Do not* use a choke collar with your Min Pin.

Your local pet shop sells an array of dishes and bowls for water and food. Since your Min Pin is such a small dog, you will only need small-sized bowls.

PHOTO COURTESY OF MIKKI PET PRODUCTS.

PUPPY-PROOFING YOUR HOME

Aside from making sure that your Miniature Pinscher will be comfortable in your home, you also have to make sure that your home is safe for your Miniature Pinscher. This means taking precautions that your pup will not get into anything he should not get into and that there is nothing within his reach that may harm him should he sniff it, chew it, inspect it, etc. This probably seems obvious since, while you are primarily concerned with your pup's safety, at the same time you do not want your belongings to be ruined. Breakables should be placed out of reach if your dog is to have full run of the house. If he is to be limited to certain places within the house, keep any potentially dangerous items in the "off-limits" areas.

An electrical cord can pose a danger should the puppy decide to taste it—and who is going to convince a pup that it would not make a great chew toy? Cords should be fastened tightly against the wall, out of puppy's sight and away from his teeth. If your dog is going to spend time in a crate, make sure that there is nothing near his crate that he can reach if he sticks his curious little nose or paws through the openings. Just as you would with a child, keep all household cleaners and chemicals where the pup cannot reach them; antifreeze is especially dangerous to dogs.

It is your responsibility to clean up after your Min Pin has relieved himself. Your local pet shop probably has devices to make the task easier.

NATURAL TOXINS

Examine your grass and landscaping before bringing your puppy home. Many varieties of plants have leaves, stems or flowers that are toxic if ingested, and you can depend on a curious puppy to investigate them. Ask your vet for information on poisonous plants or research them at your library.

If you see your dog carrying a piece of vegetation in his mouth, approach him in a quiet, disinterested manner, avoid eye contact, pet him and gradually remove the plant from his mouth. Alternatively, offer him a treat and maybe he'll drop the plant on his own accord. Be sure no toxic plants are growing in your own yard or kept in your home.

It is also important to make sure that the outside of your home is safe. Of course, your puppy should never be unsupervised, but a pup let loose in the yard will want to run and explore, and he should be granted that freedom. Do not let a fence give you a false sense of security; you would be surprised how crafty (and persistent) a dog can be in working out how to dig under and squeeze his way through small holes, or to climb over a fence. The remedy is to make the fence well embedded into the ground and high enough so that it really is impossible for your dog to get over it. Remember that the Min Pin is quite

Your Min Pin will follow his nose wherever it takes him. Aside from securely fencing your yard, make sure that nothing toxic or dangerous is contained in the areas where your Min Pin is permitted to explore.

begins, right? Well...not so fast. Something else you need to prepare is your pup's first trip to the veterinarian. Perhaps the breeder can recommend someone in the area who specializes in Toy breeds, or maybe you know some other Miniature Pinscher owners who can suggest a good vet. Either way, you should have an appointment arranged for your pup before you pick him up from the breeder.

The pup's first visit will consist of an overall examination to make sure that the pup does not have any problems that are not apparent to you. The vet will also set up a schedule for the pup's vaccinations; the breeder will inform you of which ones the pup has already received and the vet can continue from there.

nimble! Check the fence periodically to ensure that it is in good shape and make repairs as needed; a very determined pup may return to the same spot to "work on it" until he is able to get through.

FIRST TRIP TO THE VET
You have selected your puppy, and your home and family are ready. Now all you have to do is collect your Miniature Pinscher from the breeder and the fun

HOME WITH THE MANGE

Many young dogs suffer from demodectic mange, sometimes called red mange. While all breeds of dog have suffered from demodectic mange, short-coated breeds are at a greater risk. The mange manifests itself as localized infections on the face, muzzle, neck and limbs. The symptoms include hair loss and red, scaly skin. Vets routinely treat demodectic mange so that secondary infections are avoided. Many breeders remove known carriers from their programs.

INTRODUCTION
TO THE FAMILY

Everyone in the house will be excited about the puppy's coming home and will want to pet him and play with him, but it is best to make the introductions low-key so as not to overwhelm the puppy. He is apprehensive already. It is the first time he has been separated from his mother and the breeder, and the ride to your home is likely to be the first time he has been in a car. The last thing you want to do is smother him, as this will only frighten him further. This is not to say that human contact is not extremely necessary at this stage, because this is the time when a connection between the pup and his human family is formed. Gentle petting and soothing words should help console him, as well as just putting him down and letting him explore on his own (under your watchful eye, of course).

The pup may approach the family members or may busy himself with exploring for a while. Gradually, each person should spend some time with the pup, one at a time, crouching down to get as close to the pup's level as possible, letting him sniff their hands and petting him gently. He definitely needs human attention and he needs to be touched—this is how to form an immediate bond. Just remem-

Keep an eye on your ingenious little dog before he adopts horrible habits that you cannot reverse (or explain to your guests).

ber that the pup is experiencing a lot of things for the first time, at the same time. There are new people, new noises, new smells and new things to investigate, so be gentle, be affectionate and be as comforting as you can be.

Aside from his owners, the veterinarian will be your Min Pin's best friend from puppyhood throughout his life.

HOW VACCINES WORK

If you've just bought a puppy, you surely know the importance of having your pup vaccinated, but do you understand how vaccines work? Vaccines contain the same bacteria or viruses that cause the disease you want to prevent, but they have been chemically modified so that they don't cause any harm. Instead, the vaccine causes your dog to produce antibodies that fight the harmful bacteria. Thus, if your dog is exposed to the disease in the future, the antibodies will destroy the viruses or bacteria.

PUP'S FIRST NIGHT HOME

You have traveled home with your new charge safely in his crate. He's been to the vet for a thorough checkup; he's been weighed, his papers examined; perhaps he's even been vaccinated and wormed as well. He's met the whole family, including the excited children and the less-than-happy cat. He's explored his area, his new bed, the yard and anywhere else he's been permitted. He's eaten his first meal at home and relieved himself in the proper place. He's heard lots of new sounds, smelled new friends and seen more of the outside world than ever before.

That was just the first day! He's worn out and is ready for bed...or so you think! It's puppy's first night and you are

There is no limit to the amount of loving attention that a Min Pin will accept. They love people, especially children, if they have been properly socialized.

ready to say "Good night"—keep in mind that this is puppy's first night ever to be sleeping alone. His dam and littermates are no longer at paw's length and he's a bit scared, cold and lonely. Be reassuring to your new family member, but this is not the time to spoil him and give in to his inevitable whining.

Puppies whine. They whine to let others know where they are and hopefully to get company out of it. Place your pup in his new bed or crate in his room and close the crate door. Mercifully, he may fall asleep without a peep. When the inevitable occurs, ignore the whining; he is fine. Be strong and keep his future behavior in mind. Do not allow yourself to feel guilty and visit the pup. He will fall asleep eventually.

Many breeders recommend placing a piece of bedding from the pup's former home in his new bed so that he recognizes the scent of his littermates. Others still advise placing a hot-water bottle in his bed for warmth. This latter may be a good idea provided the pup doesn't attempt to suckle—he'll get good and wet, and may not fall asleep so fast.

Puppy's first night can be somewhat stressful for the pup and his new family. Remember that you are setting the tone of nighttime at your house. Unless you want to play with your pup every night at 10 p.m., midnight and 2 a.m., don't initiate the habit. Your family will thank you, and soon so will your pup!

When properly introduced, Min Pins will accept the company of the family cat. These two chums are completely comfortable in each other's company.

PUP MEETS WORLD

Thorough socialization includes not only meeting new people but also being introduced to new experiences such as riding in the car, having his coat brushed, hearing the television, walking in a crowd—the list is endless. The more your pup experiences, and the more positive the experiences are, the less of a shock and the less frightening it will be for your pup to encounter new things.

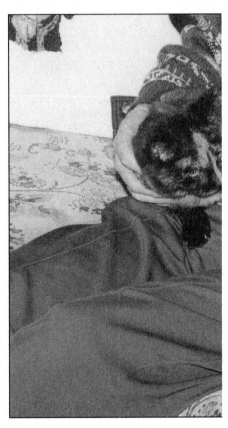

PREVENTING PUPPY PROBLEMS

SOCIALIZATION

Now that you have done all of the preparatory work and have helped your pup get accustomed to his new home and family, it is about time for you to have some fun! Socializing your Miniature Pinscher pup gives you the opportunity to show off your new friend, and your pup gets to reap the benefits of being an adorable tiny creature that

people will want to pet and, in general, think is absolutely precious!

Besides getting to know his new family, your puppy should be exposed to other people, animals and situations, but of course he must not come into close contact with dogs you

FEEDING TIPS
You will probably start feeding your pup the same food that he has been getting from the breeder; the breeder should give you a few days' supply to start you off. Although you should not give your pup too many treats, you will want to have puppy treats on hand for coaxing, training, rewards, etc. Be careful, though, as a small pup's calorie requirements are relatively low and a few treats can add up to almost a full day's worth of calories without the required nutrition.

Ouch! Your pup's very first chew toy may well be a littermate! By nipping at their siblings, pups learn just how hard they can bite without inflicting damage.

(on his lead, of course). Walk him around the neighborhood, take him on your daily errands, let people pet him, let him meet other dogs and pets, etc. Puppies do not have to try to make friends; there will be no shortage of people who will want to introduce themselves. Just make sure that you carefully supervise each meeting. If the neighborhood children want to say hello, for

don't know well until his course of injections is fully complete. Socialization will help him become well adjusted as he grows up and less prone to being timid or fearful of the new things he will encounter. Your pup's socialization began with the breeder, but now it is your responsibility to continue it. Your pup experienced a fear period between eight and ten weeks old, while still in the breeder's care. The socialization he receives in the first weeks after coming to his new home is critical, as this is the time when he forms his impressions of the outside world. Lack of socialization can manifest itself in fear and aggression as the dog grows up. He needs lots of human contact, affection, handling and exposure to other animals.

Once your pup has received his necessary vaccinations, feel free to take him out and about

STRESS-FREE
Some experts in canine health advise that stress during a dog's early years of development can compromise and weaken his immune system, and may trigger the potential for a shortened life. They emphasize the need for happy and stress-free growing-up years.

example, that is great—children and pups most often make great companions. However, sometimes an excited child can unintentionally handle a pup too roughly, or an overzealous pup can playfully nip a little too hard. You want to make socialization experiences positive ones. What a pup learns during this very formative stage will affect his attitude toward future encounters. You want your dog to be comfortable around everyone. A pup that has a bad experience with a child may grow up

"On the go" describes the ever-curious and active Min Pin pup. Be sure to stay one paw-length ahead!

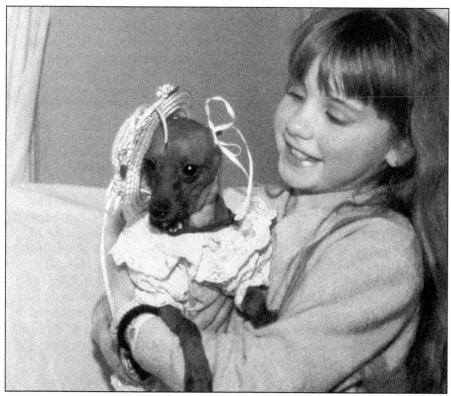

Like most other Toy breeds, Min Pins are amicably tolerant of the whims of young children to dress them up as dolls. Min Pins prefer "tea parties" where there are fancy dog biscuits to eat.

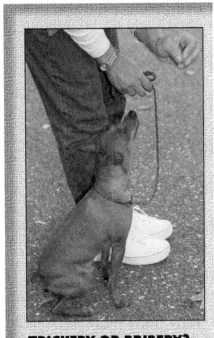

TRICKERY OR BRIBERY?
Use treats to bribe your dog into a desired behavior. Try small pieces of hard cheese or freeze-dried liver. Never offer chocolate, as it has toxic qualities for dogs.

Your pup's intuitive quest for dominance, coupled with the fact that it is nearly impossible to look at an adorable Miniature Pinscher pup with his "puppy-dog" eyes and not cave in, give the pup almost an unfair advantage in getting the upper hand! A pup will definitely test the waters to see what he can and cannot do. Do not give in to those pleading eyes—stand your ground when it comes to disciplining the pup and make sure that all family members do the same. It will only confuse the pup when Mother tells him to get off the sofa when he is used to sitting up there with Father to watch the nightly news. Avoid discrepancies by having all members of the household decide on the rules before the pup even comes home...and be consistent in enforcing them! Early training shapes the dog's personality, so you cannot be unclear in what you expect.

to be a dog that is shy around or aggressive toward children.

CONSISTENCY IN TRAINING
Dogs, being pack animals, naturally need a leader, or else they try to establish dominance in their packs. When you welcome a dog into your family, the choice of who becomes the leader and who becomes the "pack" is entirely up to you!

COMMON PUPPY PROBLEMS
The best way to prevent puppy problems is to be proactive in stopping an undesirable behavior as soon as it starts. The old saying "You can't teach an old dog new tricks" does not necessarily hold true, but it *is* true that it is much easier to discourage bad behavior in a young developing pup than to wait until the pup's bad behavior

becomes the adult dog's bad habit. There are some problems that are especially prevalent in puppies as they develop.

NIPPING

As puppies start to teethe, they feel the need to sink their teeth into anything available...unfortunately, that includes your fingers, arms, hair and toes. You may find this behavior cute for the first five seconds...until you feel just how sharp those puppy teeth are. This is something you want to discourage immediately and consistently with a firm "No!" (or whatever number of firm "Nos" it takes for him to understand that you mean business). Then replace your finger with an appropriate chew toy. While this behavior is merely annoying when the dog is young, it can become dangerous as your Miniature Pinscher's adult teeth grow in and his jaws develop, and he continues to think it is okay to nip and nibble on people. Your Miniature Pinscher does not mean any harm with a friendly nip, but he also does not know his own strength.

CRYING/WHINING

Your pup will often cry, whine, whimper, howl or make some type of commotion when he is left alone. This is basically his way of calling out for attention to make sure that you know he is there and that you have not forgotten about him. He feels insecure when he is left alone, when you are out of the house and he is in his crate or when you are in another part of the house and he cannot see you. The noise he is making is an expression of the anxiety he

PUPPY PROBLEMS
The majority of problems that are commonly seen in young pups will disappear as your dog gets older. However, how you deal with problems when he is young will determine how he reacts to discipline as an adult dog. It is important to establish who is boss (hopefully it will be you!) right away when you are first bonding with your dog. This bond will set the tone for the rest of your life together.

TRAINING TIP

Training your Min Pin takes much patience and can be frustrating at times, but you should see results from your efforts. If you have a dog that seems untrainable, take him to a trainer or behaviorist. The dog may have a personality problem that requires the help of a professional, or perhaps you need help in learning how to train your dog.

feels at being alone, so he needs to be taught that being alone is okay. You are not actually training the dog to stop making noise, you are training him to feel comfortable when he is alone and thus removing the need for him to make the noise.

This is where the crate with cozy bedding and a toy comes in handy. You want to know that the puppy is safe when you are not there to supervise, and you know that he will be safe in his crate rather than roaming freely about the house. In order for the pup to stay in his crate without making a fuss, he needs to be comfortable in his crate. On that note, it is extremely important that the crate is never used as a form of punishment, or the pup will develop a negative association with the crate.

Accustom the pup to the crate in short, gradually increasing time intervals in which you put him in the crate, maybe with a treat, and stay in the room with him. If he cries or makes a fuss, do not go to him, but stay in his sight. Gradually he will realize that staying in his crate is just fine without your help, and it will not be so traumatic for him when you are not around. You may want to leave the radio on softly when you leave the house; the sound of human voices may be comforting to him.

Acquiring a healthy puppy pays off ten-fold when it comes to the number of problem-free years you will spend with your Min Pin.

MINIATURE PINSCHER

DIETARY AND FEEDING CONSIDERATIONS

Today the choices of food for your Miniature Pinscher are many and varied. There are simply dozens of brands of food in all sorts of flavors and textures, ranging from puppy diets to those for seniors. There are even hypoallergenic and low-calorie diets available. Because your Min Pin's food has a bearing on coat, health and temperament, it is essential that the most suitable diet be selected for a Min Pin of his age. It is fair to say, however, that even experienced owners can be perplexed by the enormous range of foods available. Only understanding what is best for your dog will help you reach an informed decision.

Dog foods are produced in three basic types: dry, semi-moist and canned. Dry foods are useful for the cost-conscious, for overall they tend to be less expensive than semi-moist or canned. Dry foods also contain the least fat and the most preservatives. In general, canned foods are made up of 60–70% water, while semi-moist ones often contain so much sugar that they are perhaps the least preferred by owners, even though their dogs seem to like them.

STORING DOG FOOD

You must store your dry dog food carefully. Open packages of dog food quickly lose their vitamin value, usually within 90 days of being opened. Mold spores and vermin could also contaminate the food.

When selecting your dog's diet, three stages of development must be considered: the puppy stage, the adult stage and the senior stage.

PUPPY STAGE

Puppies instinctively want to suck milk from their mother's teats, and a normal puppy will exhibit this behavior from just a few moments following birth. If puppies do not attempt to suckle within the first half-hour or so, the breeder should encourage them to do so by placing them on the nipples, having selected ones with plenty of milk. This early milk supply is important in providing colostrum to protect the puppies during the first eight to ten weeks of their lives. Although a mother's milk is much better than any milk formula, despite there being some excellent ones available, if the puppies do not feed, the breeder will have to feed them by hand. For those with less experience, advice from a veterinarian is important so that not only the right quantity of milk but also that of correct quality is fed, at suitably frequent intervals, usually every two hours during the first few days of life.

Puppies should be allowed to nurse from their mother for about the first six weeks, although from the third or fourth week the breeder should begin to

FOOD PREFERENCE

Selecting the best dry dog food is difficult. There is no majority consensus among veterinary scientists as to the value of nutrient analysis (protein, fat, fiber, moisture, ash, cholesterol, minerals, etc.). All agree that feeding trials are what matter most, but you also have to consider the individual dog. The dog's weight, age and activity level, and what pleases his taste, all must be considered. It is probably best to take the advice of your veterinarian. Every dog has individual dietary requirements and should be fed accordingly.

If your dog is fed a good dry food, he does not require supplements of meat or vegetables. Dogs do appreciate a little variety in their diets, so you may choose to stay with the same brand but vary the flavor. Alternatively, you may wish to add a little flavored stock to give a difference to the taste.

introduce small portions of suitable solid food. Most breeders like to introduce alternate milk and meat meals initially, building up to weaning time.

By the time the puppies are seven or a maximum of eight weeks old, they should be fully weaned and fed solely on a proprietary puppy food. Selection of the most suitable, good-quality diet at this time is essential, for a puppy's fastest growth rate is during the first year of life. Vets and breeders are able to offer advice in this regard. The frequency of meals will be reduced over time as the pup reaches adulthood.

Puppy and junior diets should be well balanced for the needs of your dog, so that, except in certain circumstances, additional vitamins, minerals and proteins will not be required.

GRAIN-BASED DIETS

Some less expensive dog foods are based on grains and other plant proteins. While these products may appear to be attractively priced, many breeders prefer a diet based on animal proteins and believe that they are more conducive to your dog's health. Many grain-based diets rely on soy protein, which may cause flatulence (passing gas).

There are many cases, however, when your dog might require a special diet. These special requirements should only be recommended by your veterinarian.

ADULT DIETS

A dog is considered an adult when he has stopped growing. Take your breeder's or vet's advice as to when to switch to an adult food and the proper amounts to feed. Adult Min Pins as a rule require less food per pound of body weight than growing pups. Major dog food manufacturers specialize in adult-maintenance food, and it is merely necessary for you to select the one best suited to your dog's needs. Active dogs may have different requirements than more sedate dogs.

SENIOR DIETS

As dogs get older, their metabolism changes. The older dog usually exercises less, moves

Your breeder will start the pups off with proper nutrition, and will advise you how to continue when your pup comes home with you.

more slowly and sleeps more. This change in lifestyle and physiological performance requires a change in diet. Since these changes take place slowly, they might not be recognizable. What is easily recognizable is weight gain. By continuing to feed your dog an adult-maintenance diet when he is slowing down metabolically, your dog will gain weight. Obesity in an older dog compounds the health problems that already accompany old age.

As your dog gets older, few of his organs function up to par. The kidneys slow down and the intestines become less efficient. These age-related factors are best handled with a change in diet and a change in feeding schedule to give smaller portions that are more easily digested.

There is no single best diet for every older dog. While many dogs do well on light or senior diets, other dogs do better on puppy diets or other special premium diets such as lamb and rice. Be sensitive to your senior Miniature Pinscher's diet and this will help control other problems that may arise with your old friend.

WATER

Just as your dog needs proper nutrition from his food, water is an essential "nutrient" as well. Water keeps the dog's body prop-

FEEDING TIPS
- Dog food must be served at room temperature, neither too hot nor too cold. Fresh water, changed often and served in a clean bowl, is mandatory, especially when feeding dry food.
- Never feed your dog from the table while you are eating, and never feed your dog leftovers from your own meal. They usually contain too much fat and too much seasoning.
- Dogs must chew their food. Hard pellets are excellent; soups and stews are to be avoided.
- Don't add leftovers or any extras to commercial dog food. The normal food is usually balanced, and adding something extra destroys the balance.
- Except for age-related changes, dogs do not require dietary variations. They can be fed the same diet, day after day, without their becoming bored or ill.

DRINK, DRANK, DRUNK—MAKE IT A DOUBLE

In both humans and dogs, as well as other living organisms, water forms the major part of nearly every body tissue. Naturally, we take water for granted, but without it, life as we know it would cease.

For dogs, water is needed to keep their bodies functioning biochemically. Additionally, water is needed to replace the water lost while panting. Unlike humans, who are able to sweat to dissipate heat, dogs must pant to cool down, thereby losing the vital water that their bodies need to regulate their body temperatures. Humans lose electrolyte-containing products and other body-fluid components through sweating; dogs do not lose anything except water.

Water is essential always, but especially so when the weather is hot or humid or when your dog is exercising or working vigorously.

erly hydrated and promotes normal function of the body's systems. During house-training, it is necessary to keep an eye on how much water your Min Pin is drinking, but, once he is reliably trained, he should have access to clean fresh water at all times, especially if you feed dry food. Make certain that the dog's water bowl is clean, and change the water often.

EXERCISE

All dogs require some form of exercise, regardless of breed. A sedentary lifestyle is as harmful to a dog as it is to a person. The Min Pin is a fairly active breed that enjoys exercise, but you don't have to be an Olympic athlete to adequately exercise your dog. Exercising your Min Pin can be enjoyable and healthy for both of you. Brisk walks, once the puppy reaches three or four months of age, will stimulate heart rates and build muscle for both dog and owner. As the dog reaches adulthood, the speed and distance of the walks can be increased as long as they are both kept reasonable and comfortable for both of you. Play sessions in the yard and letting the dog run free in a fenced enclosure under your supervision also are sufficient forms of exercise for the Miniature Pinscher.

Fetching games can be played indoors or out; these are excel-

A Worthy Investment

Veterinary studies have proven that a balanced high-quality diet pays off in your dog's coat quality, behavior and activity level. Invest in premium brands for the maximum payoff with your dog.

lent for giving your dog active play that he will enjoy. If you choose to play games outdoors, you must have a securely fenced-in yard and/or have the dog

EXERCISE ALERT!
You should be careful where you exercise your dog. Many areas have been sprayed with chemicals that are highly toxic to both dogs and humans. Never allow your dog to eat grass or drink from puddles on either public or private grounds, as the run-off water may contain chemicals from sprays and herbicides.

attached to at least a 25-foot light line for security. You want your Min Pin to run, but not run away!

Bear in mind that an overweight dog should never be suddenly over-exercised; instead, he should be encouraged to increase exercise slowly. Also remember that not only is exercise essential to keep the dog's body fit, it is essential to his mental well-being. A bored dog will find something to do, which often manifests itself in some type of destructive behavior. In this sense, exercise is just as essential for the owner's mental well-being!

GROOMING

BRUSHING
With his short, shiny coat, the Miniature Pinscher almost always looks good! To help him stay well groomed, use a groomer's mitt on his coat. Running the mitt over the dog's body several times a week will remove dead hair and foreign matter from his coat. Brushing with a mitt also stimulates the oil glands in the dog's skin, thus imparting a lovely sheen to the hair.

BATHING
Dogs do not need to be bathed as often as humans; in fact, Miniature Pinschers only need to

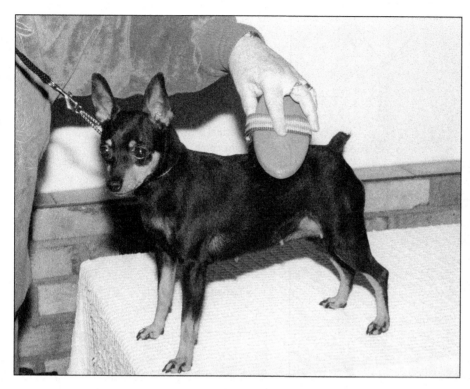

A soft bristle brush can be used on the Min Pin's coat once or twice a week.

be bathed two or three times a year. The kitchen sink is the ideal place to give your Min Pin a bath because bending down over a tub with such a tiny dog can be back-breaking for you. You should place a rubber mat or something similar in the sink so that the dog has a non-slip surface on which to stand.

Begin by wetting the dog's coat. Check the water temperature to make sure that it is neither too hot nor too cold. Use warm water and a good-quality dog shampoo (never a product made for human hair) to create a thick lather just as you would when shampooing your own hair. Wash the dog's head last; you do not want shampoo to drip into his eyes while you are washing the rest of his body. Work the shampoo all the way down to the skin. You can use this opportunity to check the skin for any bumps, bites or other abnormalities. Do not neglect any area of the body—get all of the hard-to-reach places.

Rinse thoroughly with more warm water, protecting your Min Pin's eyes from the shampoo by shielding them with your hand

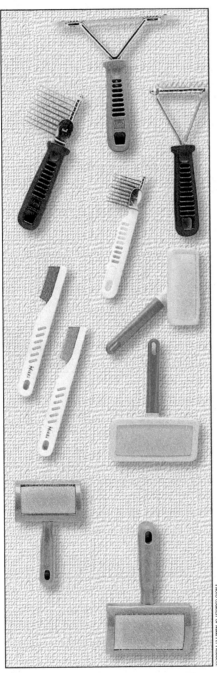

GROOMING EQUIPMENT

Invest in quality grooming tools that will last you and your Min Pin for years of use. Here are some basics:

- Groomer's mitt
- Natural bristle brush
- Flea comb
- Rubber mat
- Dog shampoo
- Coat conditioner
- Spray hose attachment
- Towels
- Ear cleaner
- Cotton balls
- Nail clippers
- Dental-care products

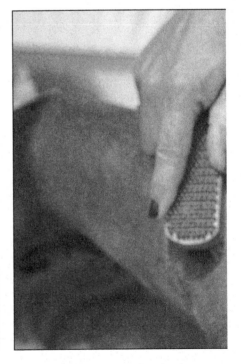

and directing the flow of water in the opposite direction. You should also avoid getting water in the ear canal. Make certain to rinse all of the shampoo from the coat, as soapy residue can be irritating to the skin. Towel-dry the coat to prevent your Min Pin from feeling chilly once the bath is over.

If desired, a final application of conditioner can give the coat a special sheen like that so often seen on show dogs. Just be certain to purchase a brand of conditioner made especially for dogs and follow the manufacturer's instructions.

SOAP IT UP
The use of human soap products like shampoo, bubble bath and hand soap can be damaging to a dog's coat and skin. Human products are too strong; they remove the protective oils coating the dog's hair and skin that make him water-resistant. Use only shampoo made especially for dogs. You may like to use a medicated shampoo, which will help to keep external parasites at bay.

Go over your Min Pin's coat with a groomer's mitt or bristle brush to remove dead hair and debris from your dog's coat and to give it a healthy shine.

EAR CLEANING
The ears should be kept clean with a cotton ball and ear-cleaning powder or liquid made especially for dogs. Be on the lookout for any signs of infection or ear-mite infestation. If your Min Pin has been shaking his head or scratching at his ears frequently, this usually indicates a problem. If his ears have an unusual odor, this is a sure sign of mite infesta-

BATHING BEAUTY

Once you are sure that the dog is thoroughly rinsed, squeeze the excess water out of his coat with your hand and dry him with an heavy towel. You may choose to use a blow dryer, on the lowest heat setting, on his coat or just let it dry naturally. In cold weather, never allow your dog outside with a wet coat.

There are "dry bath" products on the market, which are sprays and powders intended for spot cleaning, that can be used between regular baths if necessary. They are not substitutes for regular baths, but they are easy to use for touch-ups as they do not require rinsing.

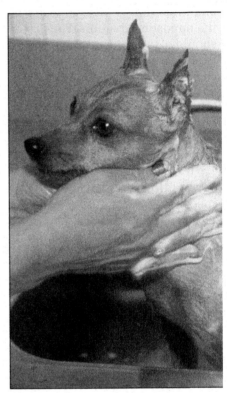

tion or infection, and a signal to have his ears checked by the veterinarian.

NAIL CLIPPING

Your Min Pin should be accustomed to having his nails trimmed at an early age, since it will be part of your maintenance routine throughout his life. Not only does it look nicer, but long nails can scratch someone unintentionally. Also, a long nail has a better chance of ripping and bleeding, or of causing the feet to spread. A good rule of thumb is

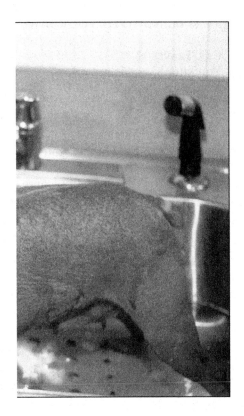

bleeding quickly when applied to the end of the cut nail. Do not panic if you cut the quick, just stop the bleeding and talk soothingly to your dog. Once he has calmed down, move on to the next nail. It is better to clip a little at a time, particularly with dark-nailed dogs like the Miniature Pinscher.

Hold your pup steady as you begin trimming his nails; you do not want him to make any sudden movements or run away. Talk to him soothingly and stroke him as you clip. Holding his foot in your hand, simply take off the end of each nail in one quick clip. You can purchase nail clippers that are specially made for dogs; you can probably find them wherever you buy pet or grooming supplies.

Min Pins, unless they become dirty, only require baths two or three times a year. The bath is easily accomplished in your kitchen sink, equipped with a non-slip mat on which the dog can stand.

Examine your Min Pin's ears regularly. Do not probe inside the ear with a cotton swab, as you may cause internal damage to the ear.

that if you can hear your dog's nails' clicking on the floor when he walks, his nails are too long.

Before you start cutting, make sure you can identify the "quick" in each nail. The quick is a blood vessel that runs through the center of each nail and grows rather close to the end. It will bleed if accidentally cut, which will be quite painful for the dog as it contains nerve endings. Keep some type of clotting agent on hand, such as a styptic pencil or styptic powder (the type used for shaving). This will stop the

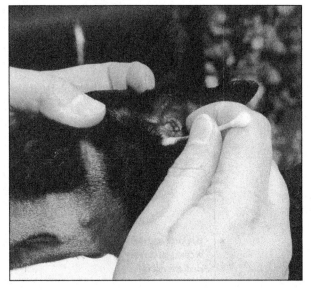

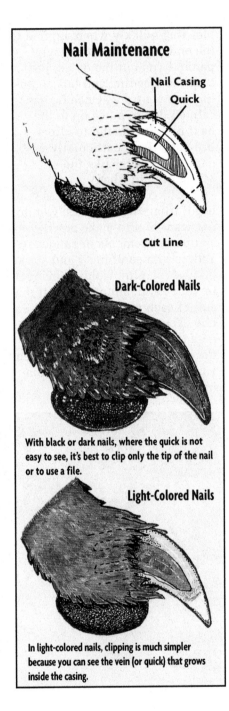

Nail Maintenance

Nail Casing

Quick

Cut Line

Dark-Colored Nails

With black or dark nails, where the quick is not easy to see, it's best to clip only the tip of the nail or to use a file.

Light-Colored Nails

In light-colored nails, clipping is much simpler because you can see the vein (or quick) that grows inside the casing.

TRAVELING WITH YOUR DOG

CAR TRAVEL

You should accustom your Miniature Pinscher to riding in a car at an early age. You may or may not take him in the car often, but at the very least he will need to go to the vet and you do not want these trips to be traumatic for the dog or troublesome for you. The safest way for a dog to ride in the car is in his crate. If he uses a crate in the house, you can use the same crate for travel.

Put the pup in the crate and see how he reacts. If he seems uneasy, you can have a passenger hold him on his lap while you drive. Another option is a specially made safety harness for dogs, which straps the dog in much like a seat belt. Do not let the dog roam loose in the vehicle—this is very dangerous! If you should stop short, your dog can be thrown and injured. If the dog starts climbing on you and pestering you while you are driving, you will not be able to concentrate on the road. It is an unsafe situation for everyone—human and canine.

For long trips, be prepared to stop to let the dog relieve himself. Take with you whatever you need to clean up after him, including some paper towels and some old rags for use should he have a potty accident in the car or suffer from motion sickness.

AIR TRAVEL

Contact your chosen airline before proceeding with travel plans that include your Miniature Pinscher. The dog will be required to travel in a fiberglass crate and you should always check in advance with the airline about specific requirements regarding the crate's size, type and labeling, as well as

It isn't difficult to learn to clip your Min Pin's nails at home. Nail clippers for dogs are sold where you buy grooming supplies.

PEDICURE TIP

A dog that spends a lot of time outside on a hard surface, such as cement or pavement, will have his nails naturally worn down and may not need to have them trimmed as often, except maybe in the colder months when he is not outside as much. Regardless, it is best to get your dog accustomed to the nail-trimming procedure at an early age so that he is used to it. Some dogs are especially sensitive about having their feet touched, but, if a dog has experienced it since puppyhood, it should not bother him.

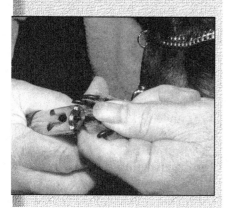

health certifications needed for the dog and any travel restrictions (such as during the summer months).

To help put the dog at ease, give him one of his favorite toys in the crate. Do not feed the dog for several hours prior to checking in so that you minimize his need to relieve himself. Some airlines require you to provide documentation as to when the dog has last been fed. In any case, a light meal is best. For long trips, you will have to attach food and water bowls to the outside of dog's crate, and a portion of food, so that airline employees can tend to him between legs of the trip.

Make sure your dog is properly identified and that your contact information appears on his ID tags and on his crate. Despite the Min Pin's small size, he is likely to be too tall to meet most airlines' specifications for in-cabin pets. Thus, your Min Pin

LET THE SUN SHINE
Your dog needs daily sunshine for the same reason people do. Pets kept inside homes with curtains drawn against the sun suffer from "SAD" (Seasonal Affected Disorder) to the same degree as humans. We now know that sunlight must enter the iris and thus progress to the pineal gland to regulate the body's hormonal system. When we live and work in artificial light, both circadian rhythms and hormone balances are disturbed.

will travel in a different area of the plane than the human passengers, so every rule must be strictly followed to prevent any risk of getting separated from your dog (although transporting pets is quite routine for major carriers).

VACATIONS AND BOARDING
So you want to take a family vacation—and you want to include *all* members of the family. You would probably make arrangements for accommodations ahead of time anyway, but this is especially important when traveling with a dog. You do not want to make an overnight stop at the only place around for miles and find out that they do

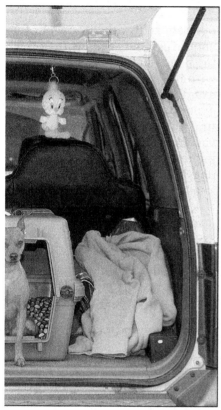

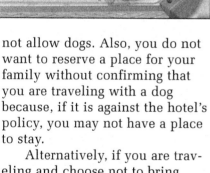

MOTION SICKNESS

*If life is a highway...*your dog may not want to come along for the ride! Some dogs experience motion sickness in cars that leads to excessive salivation and even vomiting. In most cases, your dog will fare better in the familiar, safe confines of his crate. To desensitize your dog, try going on several short jaunts before trying a long trip. If your dog experiences distress when riding in the car, drive with him only when absolutely necessary, and do not feed him or give him water before you go.

The safest and most acceptable way to travel with your Min Pin is with the dog securely in his crate.

Camping, anyone? This Min Pin is ready for a family vacation, already situated in his own tent and sleeping quarters.

not allow dogs. Also, you do not want to reserve a place for your family without confirming that you are traveling with a dog because, if it is against the hotel's policy, you may not have a place to stay.

Alternatively, if you are traveling and choose not to bring your Miniature Pinscher, you will have to make arrangements for him while you are away. Some options are to take him to a friend's house to stay while you are gone, to have a trusted neigh-

TRAVEL TIP
When traveling, never let your dog off-lead in a strange area. Your dog could run away out of fear, decide to chase a passing squirrel or cat or simply want to stretch his legs without restriction—if any of these happen, you might never see your canine friend again.

bor stop by often or stay at your house or to take your dog to a reputable boarding kennel. If you choose to board him at a kennel, you should visit in advance to see the facilities provided, how clean they are and where the dogs are kept. Talk to some of the employees and see how they treat the dogs—do they spend time with the dogs, play with them, exercise them, etc.? Do they have experience with Toy dogs? Also find out the kennel's policy on vaccinations and what they require. This is for all of the dogs' safety, since when dogs are kept together, there is a greater risk of diseases being passed from dog to dog.

IDENTIFICATION
Your Miniature Pinscher is your valued companion and friend. That is why you always keep a

Select a boarding kennel that is both conveniently located and suitable for your Min Pin. Not all facilities are ideal for small dogs.

close eye on him and you have made sure that he cannot escape from the yard or wriggle out of his collar and run away from you. However, accidents can happen and there may come a time when your dog unexpectedly gets separated from you. If this unfortunate event should occur, the first thing on your mind will be finding him. Proper identification, including an ID tag and possibly a tattoo and/or a microchip, will increase the chances of his being returned to you safely and quickly.

IDENTIFICATION OPTIONS

As puppies become more and more expensive, especially those puppies of high quality for showing and/or breeding, they have a greater chance of being stolen. The usual collar dog tag is, of course, easily removed. But there are two more permanent techniques that have become widely used for identification.

The puppy microchip implantation involves the injection of a small microchip, about the size of a corn kernel, under the skin of the dog. If your dog shows up at a clinic or shelter, or is offered for resale under less-than-savory circumstances, he can be positively identified by the microchip. The microchip is scanned, and a registry quickly identifies you as the owner.

Tattooing is done on various parts of the dog, from his belly to his ears. The number tattooed can be your telephone number, your dog's registration number or any other number that you can easily memorize. When professional dog thieves see a tattooed dog, they usually lose interest. For the safety of our dogs, no laboratory facility or dog broker will accept a tattooed dog as stock.

Discuss microchipping and tattooing with your veterinarian and breeder. Some vets perform these services on their own premises for a reasonable fee. To ensure that your dog's identification is effective, be certain that the dog is then properly registered with a legitimate national database.

As a valued friend and pet, your Miniature Pinscher deserves considerate care and proper identification. Should he become lost or stolen, you must have a reliable means to identify and find your dog.

Two ingredients
for building a
great relationship
with your Min
Pin: affection and
treats!

MINIATURE PINSCHER

Living with an untrained dog is a lot like owning a piano that you do not know how to play—it is a nice object to look at, but it does not do much more than that to bring you pleasure. Now try taking piano lessons, and suddenly the piano comes alive and brings forth magical sounds and rhythms that set your heart singing and your body swaying.

The same is true with your Miniature Pinscher. Any dog is a big responsibility and, if not trained sensibly, may develop unacceptable behavior that annoys you or could even cause family friction.

To train your Miniature Pinscher, you may like to enroll in an obedience class. Teach him good manners as you learn how and why he behaves the way he does. Find out how to communicate with your dog and how to recognize and understand his communications with you. Suddenly the dog takes on a new role in your life—he is clever, interesting, well-behaved and fun to be with. He demonstrates his bond of devotion to you daily. In other words, your

Miniature Pinscher does wonders for your ego because he constantly reminds you that you are not only his leader, you are his hero!

Those involved with teaching dog obedience and counseling owners about their dogs' behavior have discovered some interesting facts about dog ownership. For example, training dogs when they are puppies results in the highest rate of success in developing well-mannered and well-adjusted adult dogs. Training an older dog, from six months to six years of age, can produce almost equal results, providing that the

Along with a ton of training, an ounce of prevention is certainly helpful. A pup will get his paws on anything within reach, so keep your belongings out of his reach if you'd rather he didn't investigate them!

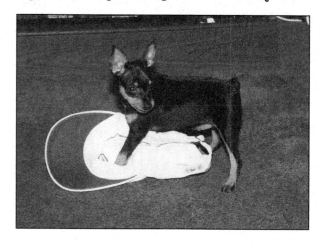

owner accepts the dog's slower rate of learning capability and is willing to work patiently to help the dog succeed at developing to his fullest potential. Unfortunately, many owners of untrained adult dogs lack the patience factor, so they do not persist until their dogs are successful at learning particular behaviors.

Training a puppy aged 10 to 16 weeks (20 weeks at the most) is like working with a dry sponge in a pool of water. The pup soaks up whatever you show him and constantly looks for more things to do and learn. At this early age, his body is not yet producing hormones, and therein lies the reason for such a high rate of success. Without

PARENTAL GUIDANCE
Training a dog is a life experience. Many parents admit that much of what they know about raising children they learned from caring for their dogs. Dogs respond to love, fairness and guidance, just as children do. Become a good dog owner and you may become an even better parent.

hormones, he is focused on his owners and not particularly interested in investigating other places, dogs, people, etc. You are his leader: his provider of food, water, shelter and security. He latches onto you and wants to stay close. He will usually follow you from room to room, will not let you out of his sight when you are outdoors with him and will respond in like manner to the people and animals you encounter. If you greet a friend warmly, he will be happy to greet the person as well. If, however, you are hesitant or anxious about the approach of a stranger, he will respond accordingly to you.

Once the puppy begins to produce hormones, his natural curiosity emerges and he begins to investigate the world around him. It is at this time when you may notice that the untrained dog begins to wander away from you and even ignore your

Jumping up at the table is certainly not acceptable behavior; enforce this rule from puppyhood by never giving in to a beggar.

commands to stay close. When this behavior becomes a problem, the owner has two choices: get rid of the dog or train him. It is strongly urged that you choose the latter option.

There will usually be classes within a reasonable distance from your home, but you can also do a lot to train your dog yourself. Sometimes there are classes available but the tuition is too costly. Whatever the circumstances, the solution to training your Min Pin without formal obedience lessons lies within the pages of this book.

This chapter is devoted to helping you train your Miniature Pinscher at home. If the recommended procedures are followed faithfully, you may expect positive results that will prove rewarding both to you and your dog.

Whether your new charge is a puppy or a mature adult, the

REAP THE REWARDS
If you start with a normal, healthy dog and give him time, patience and some carefully executed lessons, you will reap the rewards of that training for the life of the dog. And what a life it will be! The two of you will find immeasurable pleasure in the companionship you have built together with love, respect and understanding.

methods of teaching and the techniques we use in training basic behaviors are the same. After all, no dog, whether puppy or adult, likes harsh or inhumane methods. All creatures, however, respond favorably to gentle motivational methods and sincere praise and encouragement. Now let us get started.

All puppies respond to positive training techniques. It doesn't take much to inspire the attentive Min Pin puppy toward good behavior.

HOUSE-TRAINING

You can train a puppy to relieve himself wherever you choose, but this must be somewhere suitable. You should bear in mind from the outset that when your puppy is old enough to go out in public places, any canine deposits must be removed at once. You will always have to carry with you a small plastic bag or "poop-scoop."

Outdoor training includes such surfaces as grass, soil and cement. Indoor training usually means training your dog to newspaper. When deciding on the surface and location that you will want your Miniature Pinscher to use, be sure it is going to be permanent. Training your dog to grass and then changing your mind two months later is extremely difficult for both dog and owner.

Next, choose the command you will use each and every time you want your puppy to void. "Hurry up" and "Let's go" are examples of commands commonly used by dog owners. Get in the habit of giving the puppy your chosen relief command before you take him out. That way, when he becomes an adult, you will be able to determine if he wants to go out when you ask him. A confirmation will be signs of interest such as wagging his tail, watching you, going to the door, etc.

PUPPY'S NEEDS

Your puppy needs to relieve himself after play periods, after each meal, after he has been sleeping and at any time he indicates that he is looking for a place to urinate or defecate. The urinary and intestinal tract muscles of very young puppies are not fully developed. Therefore, like human babies, puppies need to relieve themselves frequently.

Take your puppy out often—every hour for a ten-week-old, for example, and always immediately after sleeping and eating. The older the puppy, the less often he will need to relieve himself. Finally, as a mature healthy adult, he will require only three to five relief trips per day.

HOUSING

Since the types of housing and control you provide for your puppy have a direct relationship on the success of house-training, we consider the various aspects of both before we begin training.

Taking a new puppy home and turning him loose in your house can be compared to turning a child loose in an amusement park and telling the child that the place is all his! The sheer enormity of the place would be too much for him to handle. Instead, offer the puppy clearly defined areas where he

CALM DOWN
Dogs will do anything for your attention. If you reward the dog when he is calm and attentive, you will develop a well-mannered dog. If, on the other hand, you greet your dog excitedly and encourage him to wrestle with you, the dog will greet you the same way and you will have a hyperactive dog on your hands.

can play, sleep, eat and live. A room of the house where the family gathers is the most obvious choice. Puppies are social animals and need to feel a part of the pack right from the start. Hearing your voice, watching you while you are doing things and smelling you nearby are all positive reinforcers that he is now a member of your pack. Usually a family room, the kitchen or a nearby adjoining breakfast area is ideal for

ATTENTION!
Your dog is actually training you at the same time you are training him. Dogs do things to get attention. They usually repeat whatever succeeds in getting your attention.

providing safety and security for both puppy and owner.

Within that room, there should be a smaller area that the puppy can call his own. An alcove, a wire or fiberglass dog crate or a partitioned (not boarded!) corner from which he can view the activities of his new family will be fine. The size of the area or crate is the key factor here. The area must be large enough for the puppy to lie down and stretch out as well as stand up without rubbing his head on the top, yet small enough so that he cannot relieve himself at one end and sleep at the other without coming into

contact with his droppings. Dogs are, by nature, clean animals and will not remain close to their relief areas unless forced to do so. In those cases, they then become dirty dogs and usually remain that way for life.

The designated area should contain clean bedding and a toy. You should avoid putting food or water in the pup's crate until he is reliably housebroken.

CONTROL

By control, we mean helping the puppy to create a lifestyle pattern that will be compatible to that of his human pack (you!). Just as we guide little children

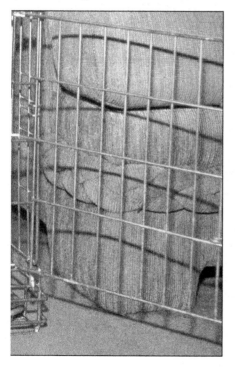

to learn our way of life, we must show the puppy when it is time to play, eat, sleep, exercise and even entertain himself.

Your puppy should always sleep in his crate. He should also learn that, during times of household confusion and excessive human activity such as at breakfast when family members are preparing for the day, he can

PAPER CAPER

Never line your pup's sleeping area with newspaper. Puppy litters are usually raised on newspaper and, once in your home, the puppy will immediately associate newspaper with voiding. Never put newspaper on any floor while house-training, as this will only confuse the puppy. If you are paper-training him, use paper in his designated relief area only. Finally, restrict water intake after evening meals. Offer a few licks at a time—never let your Min Pin gulp water after meals.

Crate training is recommended for show dogs and pet dogs alike. A wire crate provides the best ventilation and all-around view for your Min Pin.

CANINE DEVELOPMENT SCHEDULE

It is important to understand how and at what age a puppy develops into adulthood.
If you are a puppy owner, consult the following Canine Development Schedule to
determine the stage of development your puppy is currently experiencing.
This knowledge will help you as you work with the puppy in the weeks and months ahead.

Period	Age	Characteristics
FIRST TO THIRD	BIRTH TO SEVEN WEEKS	Puppy needs food, sleep and warmth, and responds to simple and gentle touching. Needs mother for security and disciplining. Needs littermates for learning and interacting with other dogs. Pup learns to function within a pack and learns pack order of dominance. Begin socializing pup with adults and children for short periods. Pup begins to become aware of his environment.
FOURTH	EIGHT TO TWELVE WEEKS	Brain is fully developed. Needs socializing with outside world. Remove from mother and littermates. Needs to change from canine pack to human pack. Human dominance necessary. Fear period occurs between 8 and 12 weeks. Avoid fright and pain.
FIFTH	THIRTEEN TO SIXTEEN WEEKS	Training and formal obedience should begin. Less association with other dogs, more with people, places, situations. Period will pass easily if you remember this is pup's change-to-adolescence time. Be firm and fair. Flight instinct prominent. Permissiveness and over-disciplining can do permanent damage. Praise for good behavior.
JUVENILE	FOUR TO EIGHT MONTHS	Another fear period about 7 to 8 months of age. It passes quickly, but be cautious of fright and pain. Sexual maturity reached. Dominant traits established. Dog should understand sit, down, come and stay by now.

NOTE: THESE ARE APPROXIMATE TIME FRAMES. ALLOW FOR INDIVIDUAL DIFFERENCES IN PUPPIES.

play by himself in relative safety and comfort in his designated area. Each time you leave the puppy alone, he should understand exactly where he is to stay.

Puppies are chewers. They cannot tell the difference between things like lamp cords, television wires, shoes, table legs, etc. Chewing into a television wire, for example, can be fatal to the puppy, while a shorted wire can start a fire in the house.

If the puppy chews on the arm of the chair when he is alone, you will probably discipline him angrily when you get home. Thus, he makes the association that your coming home means he is going to be punished. (He will not remember chewing the chair and is incapable of making the association of the discipline with his naughty deed.) Accustoming the

pup to his crate avoids his engaging in dangerous and/or destructive behaviors when you're not there to supervise.

Also, times of excitement such as family parties, friends' visits, etc., can be fun for the puppy, provided that he can view the activities from the security of his designated area. He is not underfoot and he is not being fed all sorts of tidbits that will probably cause him stomach distress, yet he still feels a part of the fun.

SCHEDULE
A puppy should be taken to his relief area each time he is released from his designated area, after meals, after play sessions and when he first awakens in the morning (at age 10 to 12 weeks, this can mean 5 a.m.!). The puppy will indicate that he's ready "to go" by circling or sniffing busily—do not misinterpret these signs. When your puppy first comes home, a routine of taking him out every hour is necessary. As

A non-spill water receptacle can be attached inside your Min Pin's crate, but this is not recommended until the puppy is completely house-trained.

the puppy grows, he will be able to wait for longer periods of time.

Keep trips to his relief area short. Stay no more than five or six minutes and then return to the house. If he goes during that time, praise him lavishly and take him indoors immediately. If he does not, but he has an accident when you go back indoors, pick him up immediately, say "No! No!" and return to his relief area. Wait a few minutes, then return to the house again. Never hit a puppy or put his face in urine or excrement when he has had an accident!

THE SUCCESS METHOD

Success that comes by luck is usually short-lived. Success that comes by well-thought-out proven methods is often more easily achieved and permanent. This is the Success Method. It is designed to give you, the puppy owner, a simple yet proven way to help your puppy develop clean living habits and a feeling of security in his new environment.

6 Steps to Successful Crate Training

1 Tell the puppy "Crate time!" and place him in the crate with a small treat (a piece of cheese or half of a biscuit). Let him stay in the crate for five minutes while you are in the same room. Then release him and praise lavishly. Never release him when he is fussing. Wait until he is quiet before you let him out.

2 Repeat Step 1 several times a day.

3 The next day, place the puppy in the crate as before. Let him stay there for ten minutes. Do this several times.

4 Continue building time in five-minute increments until the puppy stays in his crate for 30 minutes with you in the room. Always take him to his relief area after prolonged periods in his crate.

5 Now go back to Step 1 and let the puppy stay in his crate for five minutes, this time while you are out of the room.

6 Once again, build crate time in five-minute increments with you out of the room. When the puppy will stay willingly in his crate (he may even fall asleep!) for 30 minutes with you out of the room, he will be ready to stay in it for several hours at a time.

Once indoors, put the puppy in his crate until you have had time to clean up his accident. Then release him to the family area and watch him more closely than before. Chances are, his accident was a result of your not picking up his signal or waiting too long before offering him the opportunity to relieve himself. Never hold a grudge against the puppy for accidents.

Always clean up after your Min Pin has relieved himself, whether the site is a public area or your own yard.

HOW MANY TIMES A DAY?

AGE	RELIEF TRIPS
To 14 weeks	10
14–22 weeks	8
22–32 weeks	6
Adulthood	4
(dog stops growing)	

These are estimates, of course, but they are a guide to the *minimum* number of opportunities a dog should have each day to relieve himself.

Let the puppy learn that going outdoors means it is time to relieve himself, not to play. Once trained, he will be able to play indoors and out and still differentiate between the times for play versus the times for relief.

Help the pup develop regular hours for naps, being alone, playing by himself and just resting, all in his crate. Encourage him to entertain himself while you are busy with your activities. Let him learn that having you near is comforting, but it is not your main purpose in life to provide him with undivided attention.

Each time you put your puppy in his own area, use the same command, whatever suits best. Soon he will run to his crate or special area when he hears you say those words.

Crate training provides safety for you, the puppy and the home. It also provides the puppy with a feeling of security, and that helps the puppy achieve self-confidence and

method—consistency, frequency, praise, control and supervision. By following these procedures with a normal, healthy puppy, you and the puppy will soon be past the stage of "accidents" and ready to move on to a clean and rewarding life together.

ROLES OF DISCIPLINE, REWARD AND PUNISHMENT

Discipline, training one to act in accordance with rules, brings order to life. It is as simple as that. Without discipline, particularly in a group society, chaos reigns supreme and the group will eventually perish. Humans and canines are social animals and need some form of discipline in order to function effectively. They must procure food, reproduce to keep the species going and protect their home base and their young.

If there were no discipline in the lives of social animals, they would eventually die from starvation and/or predation by other

Keep training sessions happy and upbeat. Don't make the lessons too long, or your Min Pin will lose focus and interest.

clean habits. Remember that one of the primary ingredients in house-training your puppy is control. Regardless of your lifestyle, there will always be occasions when you will need to have a place where your dog can stay and be happy and safe. Crate training is the answer for now and in the future.

In conclusion, a few key elements are really all you need for a successful house-training

KEEP SMILING
Never train your dog, puppy or adult, when you are angry or in a sour mood. Dogs are very sensitive to human feelings, especially anger, and if your dog senses that you are angry or upset, he will connect your anger with his training and learn to resent or fear his training sessions.

stronger animals. In the case of domestic canines, dogs need discipline in their lives in order to understand how their pack (you and other family members) functions and how they must act in order to survive.

A large humane society in a highly populated area recently surveyed dog owners regarding their satisfaction with their relationships with their dogs. People who had trained their dogs were 75% more satisfied with their pets than those who had never trained their dogs.

Dr. Edward Thorndike, a noted psychologist, established *Thorndike's Theory of Learning*, which states that a behavior that results in a pleasant event tends to be repeated. A behavior that results in an unpleasant event tends not to be repeated. It is this theory on which training methods are based today. For example, if you manipulate a dog to perform a specific behavior and reward him for doing it, he is likely to do it again because he enjoyed the end result.

Occasionally, punishment, a penalty inflicted for an offense, is necessary. The best type of punishment often comes from an outside source. For example, a child is told not to touch the stove because he may get burned. He disobeys and touches the stove. In doing so, he

receives a burn. From that time on, he respects the heat of the stove and avoids contact with it. Therefore, a behavior that results in an unpleasant event tends not to be repeated.

A good example of a dog learning the hard way is the dog who chases the house cat. He is told many times to leave the cat

PLAN TO PLAY
Your Min Pin should also have regular play and exercise sessions when he is with you or a family member. Exercise for a very young puppy can consist of a short walk around the house or yard. Playing can include fetching games with a large ball or a special toy. (All puppies teethe and need soft things upon which to chew.) Remember to restrict play periods to indoors within his living area (the family room, for example) until he is completely house-trained.

alone, yet he persists in teasing the cat. Then, one day he begins chasing the cat but the cat turns and swipes a claw across the dog's face, leaving him with a painful gash on his nose. The final result is that the dog stops chasing the cat.

TRAINING EQUIPMENT

COLLAR AND LEAD
For a Miniature Pinscher, the collar and lead that you use for training must be one with which you are easily able to work, not too heavy for the dog and perfectly safe.

TREATS
Have a bag of treats on hand. Something nutritious and easy to swallow works best. Use a soft treat, a chunk of cheese or a piece of cooked chicken rather than a dry biscuit. By the time the dog has finished chewing a dry treat, he will forget why he

A lightweight collar is needed for the Min Pin, for both everyday walks and training sessions.

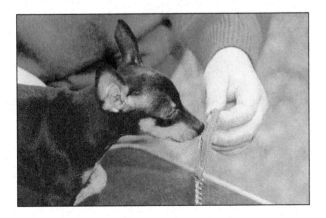

> **TRAINING RULES**
> If you want to be successful in training your dog, you have four rules to obey yourself:
> 1. Develop an understanding of how a dog thinks.
> 2. Do not blame the dog for lack of communication.
> 3. Define your dog's personality and act accordingly.
> 4. Have patience and be consistent.

is being rewarded in the first place! Using food rewards will not teach a dog to beg at the table—the only way to teach a dog to beg at the table is to give him food from the table. In training, rewarding the dog with a food treat will help him associate praise and the treats with learning new behaviors that obviously please his owner.

TRAINING BEGINS: ASK THE DOG A QUESTION
In order to teach your dog anything, you must first get his attention. After all, he cannot learn anything if he is looking away from you with his mind on something else.

To get his attention, ask him "School?" and immediately walk over to him and give him a treat as you tell him "Good dog." Wait a minute or two and repeat the routine, this time with a treat in your hand as you approach within a foot of the dog. Do not go directly to him, but stop about a foot short of him and hold out the treat as you ask "School?" He will see you approaching with a treat in your hand and most likely begin walking toward you. As you meet, give him the treat and praise again.

The third time, ask the question, have a treat in your hand and walk only a short distance toward the dog so that he must walk almost all the way to you. As he reaches you, give him the treat and praise again.

By this time, the dog will probably be getting the idea that if he pays attention to you, especially when you ask that question, it will pay off in treats and enjoyable activities for him. In

Intelligent and sensitive, Miniature Pinschers do not respond well to scolding. Be assertive and fair with your Min Pin, but never be verbally abusive to your pet, lest he'll lose heart.

LANGUAGE BARRIER

Dogs do not understand our language and have to rely on tone of voice more than just words or sound. They can be trained to react to a certain sound, at a certain volume. If you say "No, Oliver" in a very soft, pleasant voice, it will not have the same meaning as "No, Oliver!!" when you raise your voice.

You should never use the dog's name during a reprimand, just the command "No!" You never want the dog to associate his name with a negative experience or reprimand.

other words, he learns that "school" means doing great things with you that are fun and result in positive attention for him.

Remember that the dog does not understand your verbal language; he only recognizes sounds. Your question translates to a series of sounds for him, and those sounds become the signal to go to you and pay attention; if he does, he will get to interact with you plus receive treats and praise.

The sit command is easily accomplished with a tasty morsel, a firm tone of voice, a little patience and a generous helping of praise.

THE BASIC COMMANDS

TEACHING SIT

Now that you have the dog's attention, attach his lead and hold it in your left hand and a food treat in your right. Place your food hand at the dog's nose and let him lick the treat but not take it from you. Say "Sit" and slowly raise your food hand from in front of the dog's nose up over his head so that he is looking at the ceiling. As he bends his head upward, he will have to bend his knees to maintain his balance. As he bends his knees, he will assume a sit position. At that point, release the food treat and praise lavishly with comments such as "Good dog! Good sit!" etc. Remember to always praise enthusiastically, because dogs relish verbal praise from their owners and feel so proud of themselves whenever they accomplish a behavior.

Incidentally, you will not use food forever in getting the dog to obey your commands. Food is only used to teach new behaviors, and once the dog knows what you want when you give a specific command, you will wean him off the food treats but still maintain the verbal praise. After all, you will always have your voice with you, and

DOUBLE JEOPARDY

A dog in jeopardy never lies down. He stays alert on his feet because instinct tells him that he may have to run away or fight for his survival. Therefore, if a dog feels threatened or anxious, he will not lie down. Consequently, it is important to keep the dog calm and relaxed as he learns the down exercise.

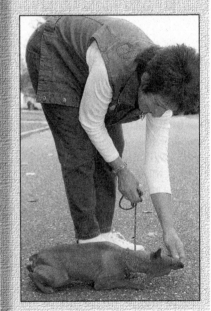

there will be many times when you have no food rewards but expect the dog to obey.

TEACHING DOWN

Teaching the down exercise is easy when you understand how the dog perceives the down position, and it is very difficult when you do not. Dogs perceive the down position as a submissive one; therefore, teaching the down exercise using a forceful method can sometimes make the dog develop such a fear of the down that he either runs away when you say "Down" or he attempts to snap at the person who tries to force him down.

Have the dog sit close alongside your left leg, facing in the same direction as you are. Hold the lead in your left hand and a food treat in your right. Now place your left hand lightly on the top of the dog's shoulders where they meet above the spinal cord. Do not push down on the dog's shoulders; simply rest your left hand there so you can guide the dog to lie down close to your left leg rather than to swing away from your side when he drops.

Now place the food hand at the dog's nose, say "Down" very softly (almost a whisper) and slowly lower the food hand to the dog's front feet. When the food hand reaches the floor, begin moving it forward along

CONSISTENCY PAYS OFF
Dogs need consistency in their feeding schedule, exercise and relief visits, and in the verbal commands you use. If you use "Stay" on Monday and "Stay here, please" on Tuesday, you will confuse your dog. Don't demand perfect behavior during training sessions and then let him have the run of the house the rest of the day. Above all, lavish praise on your pet consistently every time he does something right. The more he feels he is pleasing you, the more willing he will be to learn.

the floor in front of the dog. Keep talking softly to the dog, saying things like, "Do you want this treat? You can do this, good dog." Your reassuring tone of voice will help calm the dog as he tries to follow the food hand in order to get the treat.

When the dog's elbows touch the floor, release the food and praise softly. Try to get the dog to maintain that down position for several seconds before you let him sit up again. The goal here is to get the dog to settle down and not feel threatened in the down position.

TEACHING STAY

It is easy to teach the dog to stay in either a sit or a down position. Again, we use food and praise during the teaching

FEAR AGGRESSION

Pups who are subjected to physical abuse during training commonly end up with behavioral problems as adults. One common result of abuse is fear aggression, in which a dog will lash out, bare his teeth, snarl and finally bite someone by whom he feels threatened. For example, your daughter may be playing with the dog one afternoon. As they play hide-and-seek, she backs the dog into a corner and, as she attempts to tease him playfully, he bites her hand. Examine the cause of this behavior. Did your daughter ever hit the dog? Did someone who resembles your daughter hit or scream at the dog?

Fortunately, fear aggression is relatively easy to correct. Have your daughter engage in only positive activities with the dog, such as feeding, petting and walking. She should not give any corrections or negative feedback. If the dog still growls or cowers away from her, allow someone else to accompany them. After approximately one week, the dog should feel that he can rely on her for many positive things, and he will also be prevented from reacting fearfully towards anyone who might resemble her.

process as we help the dog to understand exactly what it is that we are expecting him to do.

To teach the sit/stay, start with the dog sitting on your left side as before and hold the lead in your left hand. Have a food treat in your right hand and place your food hand at the dog's nose. Say "Stay" and step out on your right foot to stand directly in front of the dog, toe to toe, as he licks and nibbles the treat. Be sure to keep his head facing upward to maintain the sit position. Count to five and then swing around to stand next to the dog again with him on your left. As soon as you get back to the original position, release the food and praise lavishly.

To teach the down/stay, do the down as previously described. As soon as the dog lies down, say "Stay" and step out on your right foot just as you did in the sit/stay. Count to five and then return to stand beside the dog with him on your left side. Release the treat and praise as always.

Within a week or ten days, you can begin to add a bit of distance between you and your dog when you leave him. When you do, use your left hand open with the palm facing the dog as a stay signal, much the same as the hand signal a police officer uses to stop traffic at an intersection. Hold the food treat in your right hand as before, but this time the food is not touching the dog's nose. He will watch the food hand and quickly learn that he is going to get that treat as soon as you return to his side.

When you can stand 3 feet away from your dog for 30 seconds, you can then begin building time and distance in both stays. Eventually, the dog can be expected to remain in the stay position for prolonged periods of time until you return to him or call him to you. Always praise lavishly when he stays.

TEACHING COME

If you make teaching "come" an exciting experience, you should never have a student that does not love the game or that fails to come when called. The secret, it seems, is never to teach the word "come."

At times when an owner most wants his dog to come when called, the owner is likely to be upset or anxious and he allows these feelings to come through in the tone of his voice when he calls his dog. Hearing that desperation in his owner's voice, the dog fears the results of going to him and therefore either disobeys outright or runs in the opposite direction. The secret, therefore, is to teach the dog a game and, when you want him to come to you, simply play the game. It is practically a no-fail solution!

To begin, have several members of your family take a few food treats and each go into

SAFETY FIRST
While it may seem that the most important things to your dog are eating, sleeping and chewing the upholstery on your furniture, his first concern is actually safety. The domesticated dogs we keep as companions have the same pack instinct as their ancestors who ran free thousands of years ago. Because of this pack instinct, your dog wants to know that he and his pack are not in danger of being harmed, and that his pack has a strong, capable leader. You must establish yourself as the leader early on in your relationship. That way your dog will trust that you will take care of him and the pack, and he will accept your commands without question.

a different room in the house. Take turns calling the dog, and each person should celebrate the dog's finding him with a treat and lots of happy praise. When a person calls the dog, he is actually inviting the dog to find him and get a treat as a reward for "winning."

A few turns of the "Where are you?" game and the dog will understand that everyone is playing the game and that each person has a big celebration awaiting his success at locating him or her. Once the dog learns to love the game, simply calling out "Where are you?" will bring him running from wherever he is when he hears that all-important question.

Treats are helpful in teaching all commands, including the down, the one which many dogs tend to dislike the most.

The come command is recognized as one of the most important things to teach a dog, but there are trainers who work with thousands of dogs and never teach the actual word "come." Yet these dogs will race to

> ### "COME"... BACK
> Never call your dog to come to you for a correction or scold him when he reaches you. That is the quickest way to turn a come command into "Go away fast!" Dogs think only in the present tense, and your dog will connect the scolding with coming to you, not with the misbehavior of a few moments earlier.

respond to a person who uses the dog's name followed by "Where are you?" For example, a woman has a 12-year-old companion dog who went blind, but who never fails to locate her owner when asked, "Where are you?"

Children, in particular, love to play this game with their dogs. Children can hide in smaller places like a shower stall or bathtub, behind a bed or under a table. The dog needs to work a little bit harder to find these hiding places, but, when he does, he loves to celebrate with a treat and a tussle with a favorite youngster.

TEACHING HEEL
Heeling means that the dog walks beside the owner without pulling. It takes time and patience on the owner's part to succeed at teaching the dog that he (the owner) will not proceed unless the dog is walking calmly

beside him. Pulling out ahead on the lead is definitely not acceptable. Begin by holding the lead in your left hand as the dog sits beside your left leg. Move the loop end of the lead to your right hand but keep your left hand short on the lead so it keeps the dog in close next to you. Say "Heel" and step forward on your left foot. Keep the dog close to you and take three steps. Stop and have the dog sit next to you in what we

Make training time fun time, too! Fetching games, for example, can be incorporated to reinforce the come exercise.

now call the heel position. Praise verbally, but do not touch the dog. Hesitate a moment and begin again with "Heel," taking three steps and stopping, at which point the dog is told to sit.

THE STUDENT'S STRESS TEST

During training sessions, you must be able to recognize signs of stress in your dog such as:
• tucking his tail between his legs
• lowering his head
• shivering or trembling
• standing completely still or running away
• panting and/or salivating
• avoiding eye contact
• flattening his ears back
• urinating submissively
• rolling over and lifting a leg
• grinning or baring teeth
• aggression when restrained

If your four-legged student displays these signs, he may just be nervous or intimidated. The training session may have been too lengthy, with not enough praise and affirmation. Stop for the day and try again tomorrow.

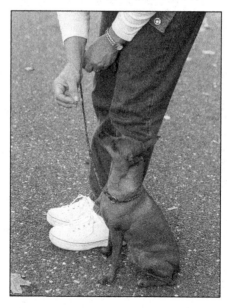

Keeping the student's attention is key to accomplishing a behavior. Min Pins are active and alert dogs, whose focus can easily stray away from the trainer who doesn't have command over his dog.

PRACTICE MAKES PERFECT!

- Have training lessons with your dog every day in several short segments—three to five times a day for a few minutes at a time is ideal.
- Do not have long practice sessions. The dog will become easily bored.
- Never practice when you are tired, ill, worried or in an otherwise negative mood. This will transmit to the dog and may have an adverse effect on his performance.

Think fun, short and above all *positive!* End each session on a high note, rather than a failed exercise, and make sure to give a lot of praise. Enjoy the training and help your dog enjoy it, too.

Your goal here is to have the dog walk those three steps without pulling on the lead. Once he will walk calmly beside you for three steps without pulling, increase the number of steps you take to five. When he will walk politely beside you while you take five steps, you can increase the length of your walk to ten steps. Keep increasing the length of your stroll until the dog will walk quietly beside you without pulling as long as you want him to heel. When you stop heeling, indicate to the dog that the exercise is over by verbally praising as you pet him and say "OK, good dog." The "OK" is used as a release word, meaning that the exercise is finished and the dog is free to relax.

If you are dealing with a dog who insists on pulling you around, simply "put on your brakes" and stand your ground until the dog realizes that the two of you are not going anywhere until he is beside you and moving at your pace, not his. It may take some time just standing there to convince the dog that you are the leader and you will be the one to decide on the direction and speed of your travel.

Each time the dog looks up at you or slows down to give a slack lead between the two of you, quietly praise him and say "Good heel. Good dog." Even-

Walking your Min Pin will be a pleasure once he has been heel-trained. This photo shows proper heeling, a behavior that must be practiced on a daily basis.

HEELING WELL
If you begin teaching the heel by taking long walks and letting the dog pull you along, he misinterprets this action as an acceptable form of taking a walk. When you pull back on the leash to counteract his pulling, he reads that tug as a signal to pull even harder!

Teach your dog to heel in an enclosed area. Once you think the dog will obey reliably and you want to attempt advanced obedience exercises such as off-lead heeling, test him in a fenced-in area so he cannot run away.

tually, the dog will begin to respond and within a few days he will be walking politely beside you without pulling on the lead. At first, the training sessions should be kept short and very positive; soon the dog will be able to walk nicely with you for increasingly longer distances. Remember also to give the dog free time and the opportunity to run and play when you have finished heel practice.

WEANING OFF FOOD IN TRAINING
Food is used in training new behaviors. Once the dog understands what behavior goes with a specific command, it is time to start weaning him off the food treats. At first, give a treat after each exercise. Then, start to give a treat only after every other exercise. Mix up the times when you offer a food reward and the times when you offer only praise so that the dog will never know when he is going to receive both food and praise and when he is going to receive only praise. This is called a variable-ratio reward system and it proves successful because there is always the chance that the owner will produce a treat, so the dog never stops trying for that reward. No matter what, *always* give verbal praise to your Miniature Pinscher.

OBEDIENCE CLASSES

It is a good idea to enroll in an obedience class if one is available in your area. If yours is a show dog, classes to prepare for the show ring would be more appropriate. Many areas have dog clubs that offer basic obedience training as well as preparatory classes for obedience competition. There are also local dog trainers who offer similar classes.

At obedience trials, dogs can earn titles at various levels of competition. The beginning levels of obedience competition include basic behaviors such as sit, down, heel, etc. The more advanced levels of competition include jumping, retrieving, scent discrimination and signal work. The advanced levels require a dog and owner to put a lot of time and effort into their training, and the titles that can be earned at these levels of competition are very prestigious.

OTHER ACTIVITIES FOR LIFE

Whether a dog is trained in the structured environment of a class or alone with his owner at home, there are many activities that can bring fun and rewards to both owner and dog once they have mastered basic control.

Teaching the dog to help in the home, in the yard or on the farm provides great satisfaction to both dog and owner. In addi-

EASY DOES IT
Gently laying your hand over the top of the dog's neck right behind the ears acts as a dominant signal. Adding a soothing, soft voice with the word "easy" can calm an overly excited dog and help him resume a normal attitude.

Even a small dog like the Min Pin will be difficult to walk if he jumps about and pulls when on lead.

is good for man and dog alike, and the bond that they develop together is priceless.

If you are interested in participating in organized competition with your Miniature Pinscher, there are activities other than obedience in which you and your dog can become involved. Agility is a popular sport in which dogs run through an obstacle course that includes various jumps, tunnels and other exercises to test the dog's speed and coordination. Min Pins are able and enthusiatic competitors. The owners run beside their dogs to give commands and to guide them through the course. Although competitive, the focus is on fun—it's fun to do, fun to watch and great exercise.

tion, the dog's help makes life a little easier for his owner and raises the dog's stature as a valued companion to his family. It helps give the dog a purpose by occupying his mind and providing an outlet for his energy.

Hiking is an exciting and healthy activity that the dog can be taught without assistance from more than his owner. The exercise of walking and climbing

A BORN PRODIGY

Occasionally, a dog and owner who have not attended formal classes have been able to earn entry-level obedience titles by obtaining competition rules and regulations from a local kennel club and practicing on their own to a degree of perfection. Obtaining the higher level titles, however, almost always requires extensive training under the tutelage of experienced instructors. In addition, the more difficult levels require more specialized equipment whereas the lower levels do not.

A well-trained
Min Pin is a
devoted
companion who
gives his owner a
lot to be proud of.

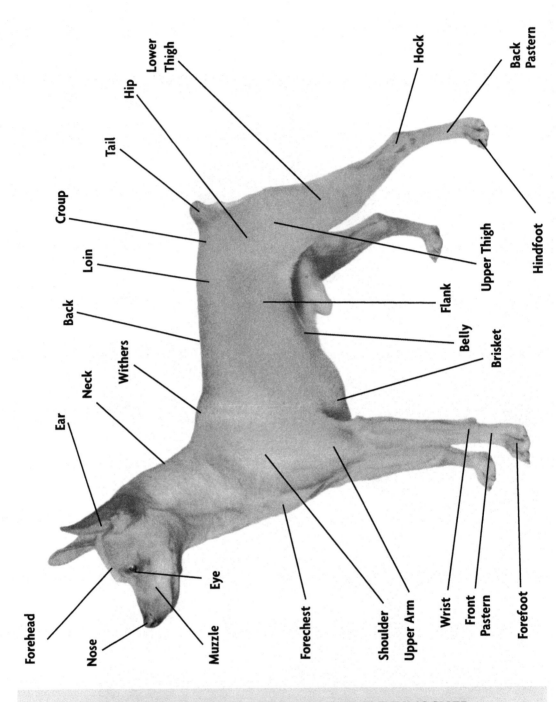

Forehead

Nose

Muzzle

Eye

Ear

Neck

Withers

Back

Loin

Croup

Tail

Hip

Lower Thigh

Hock

Back Pastern

Hindfoot

Upper Thigh

Flank

Belly

Brisket

Forechest

Shoulder

Upper Arm

Wrist

Front Pastern

Forefoot

PHYSICAL STRUCTURE OF THE MINIATURE PINSCHER

MINIATURE PINSCHER

Dogs suffer from many of the same physical illnesses as people. They might even share many of the same psychological problems. Since people usually know more about human diseases than canine maladies, many of the terms used in this chapter will be familiar but not necessarily those used by veterinarians. We will use the term *x-ray*, instead of the more acceptable term *radiograph*. We will also use the familiar term *symptoms* even though dogs don't have symptoms, which are verbal descriptions of the patient's feelings; dogs have *clinical signs*. Since dogs can't speak, we have to look for clinical signs...but we still use the term *symptoms* in this book.

As a general rule, medicine is *practiced*. That term is not arbitrary. Medicine is a constantly changing art as we learn more and more about genetics, electronic aids (like CAT scans and MRIs) and daily laboratory advances. There are many dog maladies, like hip dysplasia, which are not universally treated in the same manner. For example, some veterinarians opt for surgery more often than others do.

SELECTING A QUALIFIED VET
Your selection of a veterinarian should be based upon skills and personality as well as convenience to your home. You want a vet who is close because you might have emergencies or need to make multiple visits for treatments. You want a vet who has services that you might require such as tattooing and boarding facilities, and of course a good reputation for ability and responsiveness. There is nothing more frustrating than having to wait to receive a response from your veterinarian.

All veterinarians are licensed and capable of dealing with routine health issues like injuries, infections, routine surgeries and the promotion of health (for example, by vaccination). There are also many veterinary specialties that require further studies and internships. These include specialists in heart problems (veterinary cardiologists), skin problems (veterinary dermatologists), teeth and gum problems (veterinary dentists), eye problems (veterinary ophthalmologists) and x-rays (veterinary radiologists), as well as vets who have specialties

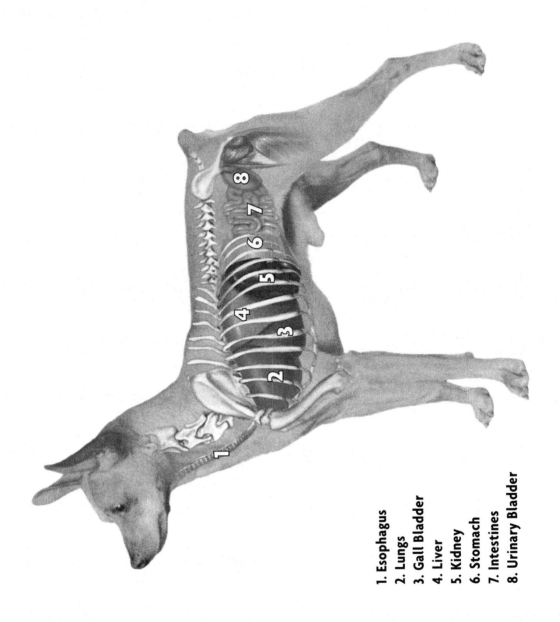

1. Esophagus
2. Lungs
3. Gall Bladder
4. Liver
5. Kidney
6. Stomach
7. Intestines
8. Urinary Bladder

INTERNAL ORGANS OF THE MINIATURE PINSCHER

in bones, muscles or certain organs. If your dog requires the help of a specialist, your veterinarian will refer you to someone in the appropriate field. When the problem affecting your dog is serious, it is not unusual or impudent to get another medical opinion, although it is courteous to advise the veterinarians concerned about this. You might also want to compare costs among several different veterinarians. Sophisticated health care and veterinary services can be very costly. If there is more than one treatment option, cost can play an important role in deciding which route to take.

PREVENTATIVE MEDICINE

It is much easier, less costly and more effective to practice preventative medicine than to fight bouts of illness and disease. Properly bred puppies come from parents who were selected based upon their genetic-disease profiles. Their mothers should have been vaccinated, free of all internal and external parasites and properly nourished. For these reasons, a visit to the veterinarian who cared for the dam is recommended. The dam can pass on disease resistance to her puppies, which can last for eight to ten weeks. She can also pass on parasites and many infections. That's why it's helpful to learn about the dam's health.

Breakdown of Veterinary Income by Category

2%	Dentistry
4%	Radiology
12%	Surgery
15%	Vaccinations
19%	Laboratory
23%	Examinations
25%	Medicines

A typical vet's income, categorized according to services performed. This survey dealt with small-animal (pets) practices.

VACCINATION SCHEDULING
Most vaccinations are given by injection and should only be done by a veterinarian. Both you and he should keep a record of the date of the injection, the identification of the vaccine and the amount given. Some vets give a first vaccination at six weeks, but most dog breeders prefer the course not to commence until about eight weeks due to risk of negating any antibodies passed on by the dam. The vaccination scheduling is usually based on a two- to four-week cycle. You must take your vet's advice regarding when to vaccinate, as this may differ according to the vaccine used.

Most vaccinations immunize your puppy against viruses. The usual vaccines contain immunizing doses of several different viruses such as distemper, parvovirus, parainfluenza and

Recognizing a Sick Dog

Unlike colicky babies and cranky children, our canine kids cannot tell us when they are feeling ill. Therefore, there are a number of signs that owners can identify to know that their dogs are not feeling well.

Take note for physical manifestations such as:
- unusual, bad odor, including bad breath
- excessive shedding
- wax in the ears, chronic ear irritation
- oily, flaky, dull haircoat
- mucus, tearing or similar discharge in the eyes
- fleas or mites
- mucus in stool, diarrhea
- sensitivity to petting or handling
- licking at paws, scratching face, etc.

Keep an eye out for behavioral changes as well, including:
- lethargy, idleness
- lack of patience or general irritability
- disinterest in food
- phobias (fear of people, loud noises, etc.)
- strange behavior, suspicion, fear
- coprophagia
- more frequent barking
- whimpering, crying

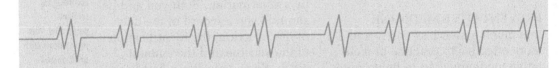

Get Well Soon

You don't need a DVM to provide good TLC to your sick or recovering dog, but you do need to pay attention to some details that normally wouldn't bother him. The following tips will aid Fido's recovery and get him back on his paws again:

- Keep his space free of irritating smells, like heavy perfumes and air fresheners.
- Rest is the best medicine! Avoid harsh lighting that will prevent your dog from sleeping. Shade him from bright sunlight during the day and dim the lights in the evening.
- Keep the noise level down. Animals are more sensitive to sound when they are sick.
- Be attentive to any necessary temperature adjustments. A dog with a fever needs a cool room and cold liquids. A bitch that is whelping or recovering from surgery will be more comfortable in a warm room, consuming warm liquids and food.
- You wouldn't send a sick child back to school early, so don't rush your dog back into a full routine until he seems absolutely ready.

hepatitis, although some vets recommend separate vaccines for each disease. There are other vaccines available when the puppy is at risk. You should rely upon professional advice. This is especially true for the booster-shot program. Most vaccination programs require a booster when the puppy is a year old and once a year thereafter. In some cases, circumstances may require more or less frequent immunizations. Canine cough, more formally known as tracheobronchitis, is treated with a vaccine that is sprayed into the dog's nostrils. Canine cough is usually included in routine vaccination, but this is often not as effective as the vaccines for other major diseases.

WEANING TO BRINGING PUP HOME
Puppies should be weaned by the time they are about two months

PARVO FOR THE COURSE

Canine parvovirus is a highly contagious disease. Spread through contact with infected feces, parvovirus causes bloody diarrhea, vomiting, heart damage, dehydration, shock and death. To prevent this tragedy, puppies should begin their series of vaccinations at six to eight weeks of age. Be aware that the virus is easily spread and is carried on a dog's hair, feet, water bowls and other objects, as well as on people's shoes and clothing.

old. A puppy that remains for at least eight weeks with his mother and littermates usually adapts better to other dogs and people later in his life.

Sometimes new owners have their puppy examined by a veterinarian immediately, which is a good idea unless the pup is over-tired by the journey home from the breeder. In that case, an appointment should be arranged for the next day.

The puppy will have his teeth examined and have his skeletal conformation and general health checked prior to certification by the veterinarian. Puppies in certain breeds have problems with their kneecaps, cataracts and other eye problems, heart murmurs and undescended testicles. Your veterinarian might also have training in temperament evaluation. The vet will set up your pup's vaccination schedule at the first visit.

FIVE TO TWELVE MONTHS OF AGE
Unless you intend to breed or show your dog, neutering or spaying the puppy around six months of age is recommended. Discuss this with your veterinarian. Neutering/spaying has proven to be extremely beneficial to both male and female dogs, respectively. Besides eliminating the possibility of pregnancy and pyometra in bitches and testicular cancer in males, it greatly reduces

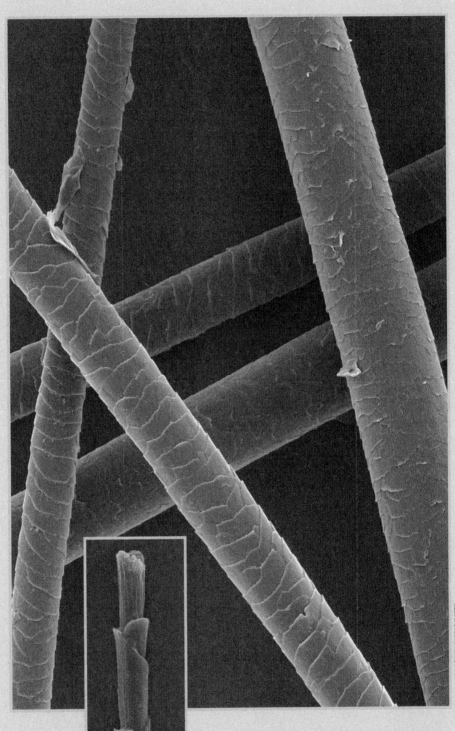

Normal hairs of a dog enlarged 200 times original size. The cuticle (outer covering) is clean and healthy. Unlike human hair that grows from the base, a dog's hair also grows from the end, as shown in the inset.

HEALTH AND VACCINATION SCHEDULE

AGE IN WEEKS:	6TH	8TH	10TH	12TH	14TH	16TH	20-24TH	52ND
Worm Control	✔	✔	✔	✔	✔	✔	✔	
Neutering							✔	
Heartworm		✔		✔		✔	✔	
Parvovirus	✔		✔		✔		✔	✔
Distemper		✔		✔		✔		✔
Hepatitis		✔		✔		✔		✔
Leptospirosis								✔
Parainfluenza	✔		✔		✔			✔
Dental Examination		✔					✔	✔
Complete Physical		✔					✔	✔
Coronavirus				✔			✔	✔
Canine Cough	✔							
Hip Dysplasia							✔	
Rabies							✔	

Vaccinations are not instantly effective. It takes about two weeks for the dog's immune system to develop antibodies. Most vaccinations require annual booster shots. Your vet should guide you in this regard.

the risk of (but does not prevent) breast cancer in bitches and prostate cancer in males.

Your veterinarian should

PUPPY VACCINATIONS

Your veterinarian will probably recommend that your puppy be fully vaccinated before you take him outside. There are airborne diseases, parasite eggs in the grass and unexpected visits from other dogs that might be dangerous to your puppy's health. Other dogs are the most harmful reservoir of pathogenic organisms, as everything they have can be transmitted to your puppy.

provide your puppy with a thorough dental evaluation at six months of age, ascertaining whether all of the permanent teeth have erupted properly. A home dental-care regimen should be initiated at six months, including brushing weekly and providing good dental devices (such as nylon bones). Regular dental care promotes healthy teeth, fresh breath and a longer life.

OLDER THAN ONE YEAR

Once a year, your grown dog should visit the vet for an examination and vaccination boosters, if

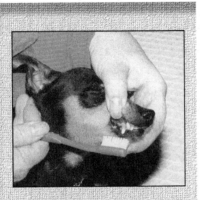

DENTAL HEALTH
A dental examination is in order when the dog is between six months and one year of age so that any permanent teeth that have erupted incorrectly can be corrected. It is important to begin a brushing routine at home, using dental-care products for dogs such as small toothbrushes and specially formulated canine toothpaste. Durable nylon and safe edible chews should be a part of your puppy's arsenal for good health, good teeth and pleasant breath. The vast majority of dogs three to four years old and older has diseases of the gums from lack of dental attention. Using the various types of dental chews can be very effective in controlling dental plaque.

needed. Some vets recommend blood tests, thyroid level check and dental evaluation to accompany these annual visits. A thorough clinical evaluation by the vet can provide critical background information for your dog. Blood tests are often performed at one year of age, and dental examinations should be part of routine check-ups. In the long run, quality preventative care for your pet can save money, teeth and lives.

SKIN PROBLEMS IN MINIATURE PINSCHERS
Veterinarians are consulted by dog owners for skin problems more than any other group of diseases or maladies. Dogs' skin is almost as sensitive as human skin and both can suffer from almost the same ailments (though the occurrence of acne in most breeds is rare). For this reason, veterinary dermatology has developed into a specialty practiced by many veterinarians.

Since many skin problems have visual symptoms that are almost identical, it requires the skill of an experienced veterinary dermatologist to identify and cure many of the more severe skin disorders. Pet shops sell many treatments for skin problems, but most of the treatments are directed at symptoms and not the underlying problem(s). If your dog is suffering from a skin disorder, you should seek professional assistance as quickly as possible. As with all diseases, the earlier a problem is identified and treated, the more likely it is that the cure will be successful.

KNOW WHEN TO POSTPONE

It is never advisable to update a vaccination when visiting the vet with a sick or pregnant dog. Vaccinations also should be avoided for all elderly dogs. If your dog is showing the signs of any illness or any medical condition, no matter how serious or mild, including skin irritations, do not vaccinate. Likewise, a lame dog should never be vaccinated; any dog undergoing surgery or on any immunosuppressant drugs also should not be vaccinated until fully recovered.

HEREDITARY SKIN DISORDERS

Veterinary dermatologists are currently researching a number of skin disorders that are believed to have hereditary bases. These inherited diseases are transmitted by both parents, who appear (phenotypically) normal but have a recessive gene for the disease, meaning that they carry, but are not affected by, the disease. These diseases pose serious problems to breeders because in some instances there is no method of identifying carriers. Often the secondary diseases associated

DISEASE REFERENCE CHART

	What is it?	What causes it?	Symptoms
Leptospirosis	Severe disease that affects the internal organs; can be spread to people.	A bacterium, which is often carried by rodents, that enters through mucous membranes and spreads quickly throughout the body.	Range from fever, vomiting and loss of appetite in less severe cases to shock, irreversible kidney damage and possibly death in most severe cases.
Rabies	Potentially deadly virus that infects warm-blooded mammals.	Bite from a carrier of the virus, mainly wild animals.	1st stage: dog exhibits change in behavior, fear. 2nd stage: dog's behavior becomes more aggressive. 3rd stage: loss of coordination, trouble with bodily functions.
Parvovirus	Highly contagious virus, potentially deadly.	Ingestion of the virus, which is usually spread through the feces of infected dogs.	Most common: severe diarrhea. Also vomiting, fatigue, lack of appetite.
Canine cough	Contagious respiratory infection.	Combination of types of bacteria and virus. Most common: *Bordetella bronchiseptica* bacteria and parainfluenza virus.	Chronic cough.
Distemper	Disease primarily affecting respiratory and nervous system.	Virus that is related to the human measles virus.	Mild symptoms such as fever, lack of appetite and mucus secretion progress to evidence of brain damage, "hard pad."
Hepatitis	Virus primarily affecting the liver.	Canine adenovirus type I (CAV-1). Enters system when dog breathes in particles.	Lesser symptoms include listlessness, diarrhea, vomiting. More severe symptoms include "blue-eye" (clumps of virus in eye).
Coronavirus	Virus resulting in digestive problems.	Virus is spread through infected dog's feces.	Stomach upset evidenced by lack of appetite, vomiting, diarrhea.

with these skin conditions are even more debilitating than the disorder itself, including cancers and respiratory problems.

Among the hereditary skin disorders, for which the mode of inheritance is known, are color dilution alopecia, a problem in in blue-gray or fawn Min Pins, acrodermatitis, cutaneous asthenia (Ehlers-Danlos syndrome), sebaceous adenitis, cyclic hematopoiesis, dermatomyositis, IgA deficiency and nodular dermatofibrosis. Some of these disorders are limited to one or two breeds and others affect a large number of breeds. All inherited diseases must be diagnosed and treated by a veterinary specialist.

PARASITE BITES

Many of us are allergic to insect bites. The bites itch, erupt and may even become infected. Dogs have the same reaction to fleas, ticks and/or mites. When an insect lands on you, you have the chance to whisk it away with your hand. Unfortunately, when your

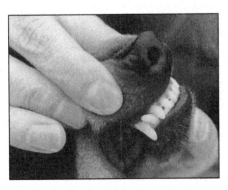

You should examine your Min Pin's teeth regularly. Brushing on a weekly basis usually suffices for dental health care at home.

> ### "P" STANDS FOR PROBLEM
> Urinary-tract disease is a serious condition that requires immediate medical attention. Symptoms include urinating in inappropriate places or the need to urinate frequently in small amounts. Urinary-tract disease is most effectively treated with antibiotics. To help promote good urinary-tract health, owners must always be sure that a constant supply of fresh water is available to their pets.

dog is bitten by a flea, tick or mite, he can only scratch it away or bite it. By the time the dog has been bitten, the parasite has done some of its damage. It may also have laid eggs to cause further problems in the near future. The itching from parasite bites is probably due to the saliva injected into the site when the parasite sucks the dog's blood.

AUTO-IMMUNE SKIN CONDITIONS

Auto-immune skin conditions are commonly referred to as being allergic to yourself, while allergies are usually inflammatory reactions to outside stimuli. Auto-immune diseases cause serious damage to the tissues that are involved.

The best known auto-immune disease is lupus, which affects people as well as dogs. The symptoms are variable and may affect

First Aid at a Glance

Burns
Place the affected area under cool water; use ice if only a small area is burnt.

Bee stings/Insect bites
Apply ice to relieve swelling; antihistamine dosed properly.

Animal bites
Clean any bleeding area; apply pressure until bleeding subsides; go to the vet.

Spider bites
Use cold compress and a pressurized pack to inhibit venom's spreading.

Antifreeze poisoning
Induce vomiting with hydrogen peroxide. Seek *immediate* veterinary help!

Fish hooks
Removal best handled by vet; hook must be cut in order to remove.

Snake bites
Pack ice around bite; contact vet quickly; identify snake for proper antivenin.

Car accident
Move dog from roadway with blanket; seek veterinary aid.

Shock
Calm the dog; keep him warm; seek immediate veterinary help.

Nosebleed
Apply cold compress to the nose; apply pressure to any visible abrasion.

Bleeding
Apply pressure above the area; treat wound by applying a cotton pack.

Heat stroke
Submerge dog in cold bath; cool down with fresh air and water; go to the vet.

Frostbite/Hypothermia
Warm the dog with a warm bath, electric blankets or hot water bottles.

Abrasions
Clean the wound and wash out thoroughly with fresh water; apply antiseptic.

 Remember: an injured dog may attempt to bite a helping hand from fear and confusion. Always muzzle the dog before trying to offer assistance.

the kidneys, bones, blood chemistry and skin. It can be fatal to both dogs and humans, though it is not thought to be transmissible. It is usually successfully treated with cortisone, prednisone or a similar corticosteroid, but extensive use of these drugs can have harmful side effects.

AIRBORNE ALLERGIES

An interesting allergy is pollen allergy. Just as humans have hay fever, rose fever and other fevers with which they suffer during the pollinating season, many dogs suffer from the same allergies. When the pollen count is high, your dog might suffer, but don't expect him to sneeze and have a runny nose like a human would. Dogs react to pollen allergies the same way they react to fleas—they scratch and bite themselves.

Dogs, like humans, can be tested for allergens. Discuss the testing with your veterinary dermatologist.

FOOD PROBLEMS

FOOD ALLERGIES

Dogs are allergic to many foods that may be best-sellers and highly recommended by breeders and veterinarians. Changing the brand of food that you buy may not eliminate the problem if the element to which the dog is allergic is contained in the new brand.

Recognizing a food allergy is

PROPER DIET
Feeding your dog properly is very important. An incorrect diet could affect the dog's health, behavior and nervous system, possibly making a normal dog into an aggressive one. Its most visible effects are to the skin and coat, but internal organs are similarly affected.

difficult. Humans usually vomit or have rashes when they eat a food to which they are allergic. Dogs neither vomit nor (usually) develop a rash. They react in the same manner as they do to an airborne or flea allergy; they itch, scratch and bite, thus making the diagnosis extremely difficult. While pollen allergies and parasite bites are usually seasonal, food allergies are year-round problems.

FOOD INTOLERANCE

Food intolerance is the inability of the dog to completely digest certain foods. For example, puppies that may have done very well on their mother's milk may not do well on cow's milk. The result of this food intolerance may be loose bowels, passing gas and stomach pains. These are the only obvious symptoms of food intolerance, which makes diagnosis difficult since these symptoms can be indicative of various other problems, too.

TREATING FOOD PROBLEMS

It is possible to handle food allergies and food intolerance yourself. Put your dog on a diet that he has never had. Obviously, if he has never eaten this new food, he can't have been allergic or intolerant of it. Start with a single ingredient that is not in the dog's diet at the present time. Ingredients like chopped beef or chicken are common in dogs' diets, so try another protein source like fish or lamb, or even something more exotic like rabbit or pheasant. Keep the dog on this diet (with no additives) for a month. If the symptoms of food allergy or intolerance disappear, chances are your dog has a food allergy.

Don't think that the single ingredient cured the problem. You still must find a suitable diet and ascertain which ingredient in the old diet was objectionable. This is most easily done by adding ingredients to the new diet one at a time. Let the dog stay on the modified diet for a month before you add another ingredient. Eventually, you will determine the ingredient that caused the adverse reaction.

An alternative method is to carefully study the ingredients in the diet to which your dog is allergic or intolerant. Identify the main ingredient in this diet and eliminate it by buying a different food that does not have that ingredient. Keep experimenting until the symptoms disappear after one month on the new diet.

PET ADVANTAGES

If you do not intend to show or breed your new puppy, your veterinarian will probably recommend that you spay your female or neuter your male. Male dogs are castrated. The operation removes both testicles and requires that the dog be anesthetized. Recovery takes about one week. Females are spayed; in this operation, the uterus (womb) and both of the ovaries are removed. This is major surgery, also carried out under general anesthesia, and it usually takes a bitch two weeks to recover.

Some people believe neutering leads to weight gain, but if you feed and exercise your dog properly, this is easily avoided. Spaying or neutering can actually have many positive outcomes, such as:

- training becomes easier, as the dog focuses less on the urge to mate and more on you!
- females are protected from unplanned pregnancy as well as ovarian and uterine cancers.
- males are guarded from testicular tumors and have a reduced risk of developing prostate cancer.

Talk to your vet regarding the right age to spay/neuter and other aspects of the procedure.

A scanning electron micrograph of a dog flea, *Ctenocephalides canis,* on dog hair.

EXTERNAL PARASITES

FLEAS

Fleas have been around for millions of years and, while we have better tools now for controlling them than at any time in the past, there still is little chance that they will end up on an endangered species list. Actually, they are very well adapted to living on our pets, and they continue to adapt as we make advances.

The female flea can consume 15 times her weight in blood during active reproduction and can lay as many as 40 eggs a day. These eggs are very resistant to the effects of insecticides. They hatch into larvae, which then mature and spin cocoons. The immature fleas reside in this pupal stage until the time is right for feeding. This pupal stage is also very resistant to the effects of insecticides, and pupae can last in the environment without feeding for many months. Newly emergent fleas are attracted to animals by the warmth of the animals' bodies, movement and exhaled carbon dioxide. However, when they first emerge from their cocoons, they orient towards light; thus when an animal passes between a flea and the light source, casting a shadow, the flea pounces and starts to feed. If the animal turns out to be a dog or cat, the reproductive cycle continues. If the flea lands on another type of animal, including a person, the flea will bite but will then look for a more appropriate host. An emerging adult flea can survive without feeding for up to 12 months but, once it tastes blood, it can survive off its host for only three to four days.

It was once thought that fleas spend most of their lives in the environment, but we now know that fleas won't willingly jump off a dog unless leaping to another dog or when physically removed by brushing, bathing or other manipulation. Flea eggs, on the other hand, are shiny and smooth, and they roll off the animal and into the environment. The eggs, larvae and pupae then exist in the environment, but once the adult finds a susceptible animal, it's home sweet home until the flea is forced to seek refuge elsewhere.

Since adult fleas live on the animal and immature forms survive in the environment, a successful treatment plan must address all stages of the flea life cycle. There are now several safe and effective flea-control products that can be applied on a monthly

FLEA PREVENTION FOR YOUR DOG
- Discuss with your veterinarian the safest product to protect your dog, likely in the form of a monthly tablet or a liquid preparation placed on the back of the dog's neck.
- For dogs suffering from flea-bite dermatitis, a shampoo or topical insecticide treatment is required.
- Your lawn and property should be sprayed with an insecticide designed to kill fleas and ticks that lurk outdoors.
- Using a flea comb, check the dog's coat regularly for any signs of parasites.
- Practice good housekeeping. Vacuum floors, carpets and furniture regularly, especially in the areas that the dog frequents, and wash the dog's bedding weekly.
- Follow up house-cleaning with carpet shampoos and sprays to rid the house of fleas at all stages of development. Insect growth regulators are the safest option.

basis. These include fipronil, imidacloprid, selamectin and permethrin (found in several formulations). Most of these products have significant flea-killing rates within 24 hours. However, none of them will control the immature forms in the environment. To accomplish this, there are a variety of insect growth regulators that can be

THE FLEA'S LIFE CYCLE

What came first, the flea or the egg? This age-old mystery is more difficult to comprehend than the actual cycle of the flea. Fleas usually live only about four months. A female can lay 2,000 eggs in her lifetime.

PHOTO BY CAROLINA BIOLOGICAL SUPPLY CO.

Egg

After ten days of rolling around your carpet or under your furniture, the eggs hatch into larvae, which feed on various and sundry debris. In days or months, depending on the climate, the larvae spin cocoons and develop into the pupal or nymph stage, which quickly develop into fleas.

Larva

PHOTO BY CAROLINA BIOLOGICAL SUPPLY CO.

Pupa

These immature fleas must locate a host within 10 to 14 days or they will die. Only about 1% of the flea population exist as adult fleas, while the other 99% exist as eggs, larvae or pupae.

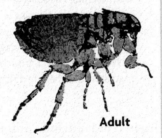

Adult

KILL FLEAS THE NATURAL WAY

If you choose not to go the route of conventional medication, there are some natural ways to ward off fleas:

• Dust your dog with a natural flea powder, composed of such herbal goodies as rosemary, wormwood, pennyroyal, citronella, rue, tobacco powder and eucalyptus.

• Apply diatomaceous earth, the fossilized remains of single-cell algae, to your carpets, furniture and pet's bedding. Even though it's not good for dogs, it's even worse for fleas, which will dry up swiftly and die.

• Brush your dog frequently, give him adequate exercise and let him fast occasionally. All of these activities strengthen the dog's system and make him more resistant to disease and parasites.

• Bathe your dog with a capful of pennyroyal or eucalyptus oil.

• Feed a natural diet, free of additives and preservatives. Add some fresh garlic and brewer's yeast to the dog's morning portion, as these items have flea-repelling properties.

sprayed into the environment (e.g., pyriproxyfen, methoprene, fenoxycarb) as well as insect development inhibitors such as lufenuron that can be administered. These compounds have no effect on adult fleas, but they stop immature forms from developing into adults. In years gone by, we relied heavily on toxic insecticides (such as organophosphates, organochlorines and carbamates) to manage the flea problem, but today's options are not only much safer to use on our pets but also safer for the environment.

TICKS

Ticks are members of the spider class (arachnids) and are blood-sucking parasites capable of transmitting a variety of diseases, including Lyme disease, ehrlichiosis, babesiosis and Rocky Mountain spotted fever. It's easy to see ticks on your own skin, but it is more of a challenge when your dog is affected. Whenever you happen to be planning a stroll in a tick-infested area (especially forests, grassy or wooded areas or parks) be prepared to do a thorough inspection of your dog afterward to search for ticks. Ticks can be tricky, so make sure you spend time looking in the ears, between the toes and everywhere else where a tick might hide. Ticks need to be attached for 24–72 hours before they transmit most of the diseases that they carry, so you do have a window of opportunity for some preventive intervention.

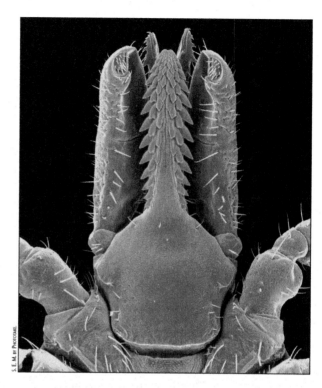

A scanning electron micrograph of the head of a female deer tick, *Ixodes dammini*, a parasitic tick that carries Lyme disease.

Female ticks live to eat and breed. They can lay between 4,000 and 5,000 eggs and they die soon after. Males, on the other hand, live only to mate with the females and continue the process as long as they are able. Most ticks live on multiple hosts before parasitizing dogs. The immature forms typically reside on grass and shrubs, waiting for susceptible animals to walk by. The larvae and nymph stages typically feed on wildlife.

If only a few ticks are present on a dog, they can be plucked out, but it is important to remove the entire head and mouthparts,

A TICKING BOMB

There is nothing good about a tick's harpooning his nose into your dog's skin. Among the diseases caused by ticks are Rocky Mountain spotted fever, canine ehrlichiosis, canine babesiosis, canine hepatozoonosis and Lyme disease. If a dog is allergic to the saliva of a female wood tick, he can develop tick paralysis.

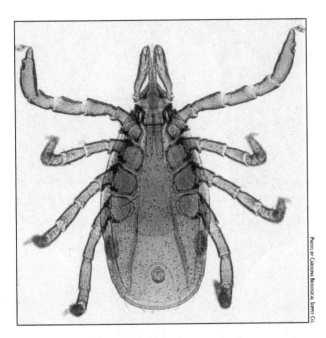

PHOTO BY CAROLINA BIOLOGICAL SUPPLY CO.

Deer tick, Ixodes dammini.

disposed of in a container of alcohol or household bleach.

Some of the newer flea products, specifically those with fipronil, selamectin and permethrin, have effect against some, but not all, species of tick. Flea collars containing appropriate pesticides (e.g., propoxur, chlorfenvinphos) can aid in tick control. In most areas, such collars should be placed on animals in March, at the beginning of the tick season, and changed regularly. Leaving the collar on when the pesticide level is waning invites the development of resistance. Amitraz collars are also good for tick control, and the active ingredient does not interfere with other flea-control products. The ingredient helps prevent the attachment of ticks to the skin and will cause those ticks already on the skin to detach themselves.

which may be deeply embedded in the skin. This is best accomplished with forceps designed especially for this purpose; fingers can be used but should be protected with rubber gloves, plastic wrap or at least a paper towel. The tick should be grasped as closely as possible to the animal's skin and should be pulled upward with steady, even pressure. Do not squeeze, crush or puncture the body of the tick or you risk exposure to any disease carried by that tick. Once the ticks have been removed, the sites of attachment should be disinfected. Your hands should then be washed with soap and water to further minimize risk of contagion. The tick should be

TICK CONTROL

Removal of underbrush and leaf litter and the thinning of trees in areas where tick control is desired are recommended. These actions remove the cover and food sources for small animals that serve as hosts for ticks. With continued mowing of grasses in these areas, the probability of ticks' surviving is further reduced. A variety of insecticide ingredients (e.g., resmethrin, carbaryl, permethrin, chlorpyrifos, dioxathion and allethrin) are registered for tick control around the home.

MITES

Mites are tiny arachnid parasites that parasitize the skin of dogs. Skin diseases caused by mites are referred to as "mange," and there are many different forms seen in dogs. These forms are very different from one another, each one warranting an individual description.

Sarcoptic mange, or scabies, is one of the itchiest conditions that affects dogs. The microscopic *Sarcoptes* mites burrow into the superficial layers of the skin and can drive dogs crazy with itchiness. They are also communicable to people, although they can't complete their reproductive cycle on people. In addition to being tiny, the mites also are often difficult to find when trying to make a diagnosis. Skin scrapings from multiple areas are examined microscopically but, even then, sometimes the mites cannot be found.

Fortunately, scabies is relatively easy to treat, and there are a variety of products that will successfully kill the mites. Since the mites can't live in the environment for very long without feeding, a complete cure is usually possible within four to eight weeks.

Cheyletiellosis is caused by a relatively large mite, which sometimes can be seen even without a microscope. Often referred to as "walking dandruff," this also causes itching, but not usually as profound as with scabies.

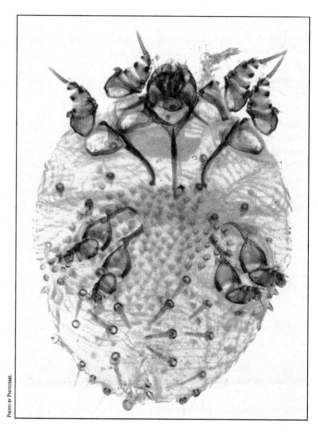

PHOTO BY PHOTOTAKE.

Sarcoptes scabiei, commonly known as the "itch mite."

While *Cheyletiella* mites can survive somewhat longer in the environment than scabies mites, they too are relatively easy to treat, being responsive to not only the medications used to treat scabies but also often to flea-control products.

Otodectes cynotis is the canine ear mite and is one of the more common causes of mange, especially in young dogs in shelters or pet stores. That's because the mites are typically present in large numbers and are quickly spread to

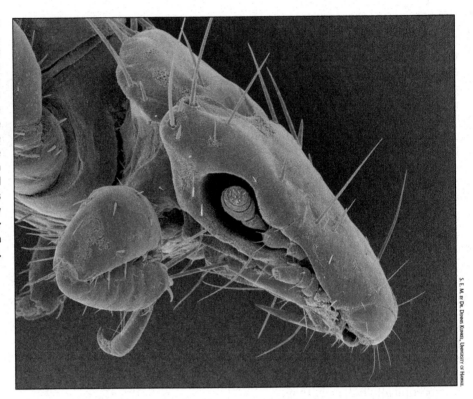

Micrograph of a dog louse, *Heterodoxus spiniger*. Female lice attach their eggs to the hairs of the dog. As the eggs hatch, the larval lice bite and feed on the blood. Lice can also feed on dead skin and hair. This feeding activity can cause hair loss and skin problems.

nearby animals. The mites rarely do much harm but can be difficult to eradicate if the treatment regimen is not comprehensive. While many try to treat the condition with ear drops only, this is the most common cause of treatment failure. Ear drops cause the mites to simply move out of the ears and as far away as possible (usually to the base of the tail) until the insecticide levels in the ears drop to an acceptable level—then it's back to business as usual! The successful treatment of ear mites requires treating all animals in the household with a systemic insecticide, such as selamectin, or a combination of miticidal ear drops combined with whole-body flea-control preparations.

Demodicosis, sometimes referred to as red mange, is sometimes a difficult problem in dogs and can be one of the most difficult forms of mange to treat. Part of the problem has to do with the fact that the mites live in the hair follicles and they are relatively well shielded from topical and systemic products. The main issue, however, is that demodectic mange typically results only when there is some underlying process interfering with the dog's immune system.

Since *Demodex* mites are normal residents of the skin of mammals, including humans, there is usually a mite population explosion only when the immune system fails to keep the number of mites in check. In young animals, the immune deficit may be transient or may reflect an actual inherited immune problem. In older animals, demodicosis is usually seen only when there is another disease hampering the immune system, such as diabetes, cancer, thyroid problems or the use of immune-suppressing drugs. Accordingly, treatment involves not only trying to kill the mange mites but also discerning what is interfering with immune function and correcting it if possible.

Chiggers represent several different species of mite that don't parasitize dogs specifically, but do latch on to passersby and can cause irritation. The problem is most prevalent in wooded areas in the late summer and fall. Treatment is not difficult, as the mites do not complete their life cycle on dogs and are susceptible to a variety of miticidal products.

MOSQUITOES

Mosquitoes have long been known to transmit a variety of diseases to people, as well as just being biting pests during warm weather. They also pose a real risk to pets. Not only do they carry deadly heartworms but recently there also has been much concern over their involvement with West Nile virus. While we can avoid heartworm with the use of preventive medications, there are no such preventives for West Nile virus. The only method of prevention in endemic areas is active mosquito control. Fortunately, most dogs that have been exposed to the virus only developed flu-like symptoms and, to date, there have not been the large number of reported deaths in canines as seen in some other species.

ILLUSTRATION BY PHOTOTAKE

Illustration of *Demodex folliculoram*.

MOSQUITO REPELLENT

Low concentrations of DEET (less than 10%), found in many human mosquito repellents, have been safely used in dogs but, in these concentrations, probably give only about two hours of protection. DEET may be safe in these small concentrations, but since it is not licensed for use on dogs, there is no research proving its safety for dogs. Products containing permethrin give the longest-lasting protection, perhaps two to four weeks. As DEET is not licensed for use on dogs, and both DEET and permethrin can be quite toxic to cats, appropriate care should be exercised. Other products, such as those containing oil of citronella, also have some mosquito-repellent activity, but typically have a relatively short duration of action.

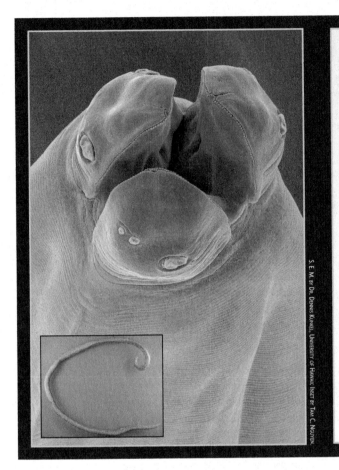

S. E. M. BY DR. DENNIS KUNKEL, UNIVERSITY OF HAWAII; INSET BY TAM C. NGUYEN.

The ascarid roundworm *Toxocara canis,* showing the mouth with three lips. INSET: Photomicrograph of the roundworm *Ascaris lumbricoides.*

INTERNAL PARASITES: WORMS

ASCARIDS

Ascarids are intestinal roundworms that rarely cause severe disease in dogs. Nonetheless, they are of major public health significance because they can be transferred to people. Sadly, it is children who are most commonly affected by the parasite, probably from inadvertently ingesting ascarid-contaminated soil. In fact, many yards and children's sandboxes contain appreciable numbers of ascarid eggs. So, while ascarids don't bite dogs or latch onto their intestines to suck blood, they do cause some nasty medical conditions in children and are best eradicated from our furry friends. Because pups can start passing ascarid eggs by three weeks of age, most parasite-control programs begin at two weeks of age and are repeated every two weeks until pups are eight weeks old. It is important to

HOOKED ON *ANCYLOSTOMA*

Adult dogs can become infected by the bloodsucking nematodes we commonly call hookworms via ingesting larvae from the ground or via the larvae penetrating the dog's skin. It is not uncommon for infected dogs to show no symptoms of hookworm infestation. Sometimes symptoms occur within ten days of exposure. These symptoms can include bloody diarrhea, anemia, loss of weight and general weakness. Dogs pass the hookworm eggs in their stools, which serves as the vet's method of identifying the infestation. The hookworm larvae can encyst themselves in the dog's tissues and be released when the dog is experiencing stress.

Caused by an *Ancylostoma* species whose common host is the dog, cutaneous larval migrans affects humans, causing itching and lumps and streaks beneath the surface of the skin.

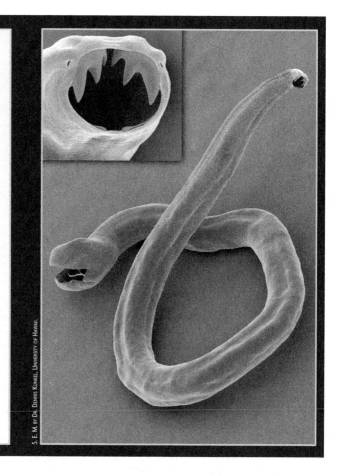

S. E. M. BY DR. DENNIS KUNKEL, UNIVERSITY OF HAWAII.

realize that bitches can pass ascarids to their pups even if they test negative prior to whelping. Accordingly, bitches are best treated at the same time as the pups.

HOOKWORMS

Unlike ascarids, hookworms do latch onto a dog's intestinal tract and can cause significant loss of blood and protein. Similar to ascarids, hookworms can be transmitted to humans, where they cause a condition known as cutaneous larval migrans. Dogs can become infected either by consuming the infective larvae or by the larvae's penetrating the skin directly. People most often get infected when they are lying on the ground (such as on a beach) and the larvae penetrate the skin. Yes, the larvae can penetrate through a beach blanket. Hookworms are typically susceptible to the same medications used to treat ascarids.

The hookworm *Ancylostoma caninum* infests the intestines of dogs. INSET: Note the row of hooks at the posterior end, used to anchor the worm to the intestinal wall.

WHIPWORMS

Whipworms latch onto the lower aspects of the dog's colon and can cause cramping and diarrhea. Eggs do not start to appear in the dog's feces until about three months after the dog was infected. This worm has a peculiar life cycle, which makes it more difficult to control than ascarids or hookworms. The good thing is that whipworms rarely are transferred to people.

Some of the medications used to treat ascarids and hookworms are also effective against whipworms, but, in general, a separate treatment protocol is needed. Since most of the medications are effective against the adults but not the eggs or larvae, treatment is typically repeated in three weeks, and then often in three

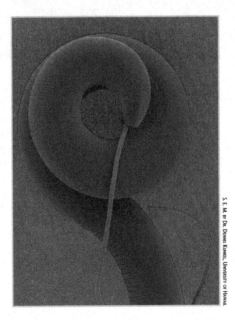

Adult whipworm, *Trichuris* sp., an intestinal parasite.

S. E. M. BY DR. DENNIS KUNKEL, UNIVERSITY OF HAWAII

WORM-CONTROL GUIDELINES

• Practice sanitary habits with your dog and home.
• Clean up after your dog and don't let him sniff or eat other dogs' droppings.
• Control insects and fleas in the dog's environment. Fleas, lice, cockroaches, beetles, mice and rats can act as hosts for various worms.
• Prevent dogs from eating uncooked meat, raw poultry and dead animals.
• Keep dogs and children from playing in sand and soil.
• Kennel dogs on cement or gravel; avoid dirt runs.
• Administer heartworm preventives regularly.
• Have your vet examine your dog's stools at your annual visits.
• Select a boarding kennel carefully so as to avoid contamination from other dogs or an unsanitary environment.
• Prevent dogs from roaming. Obey local leash laws.

---

months as well. Unfortunately, since dogs don't develop resistance to whipworms, it is difficult to prevent them from getting reinfected if they visit soil contaminated with whipworm eggs.

TAPEWORMS

There are many different species of tapeworm that affect dogs, but *Dipylidium caninum* is probably the most common and is spread by fleas. Flea larvae feed on organic debris and tapeworm eggs in the environment and, when a dog chews at himself and manages to ingest fleas, he might get a dose of tapeworm at the same time. The tapeworm then develops further in the intestine of the dog.

The tapeworm itself, which is a parasitic flatworm that latches onto the intestinal wall, is composed of numerous segments. When the segments break off into the intestine (as proglottids), they may accumulate around the rectum, like grains of rice. While this tapeworm is disgusting in its behavior, it is not directly communicable to humans (although humans can also get infected by swallowing fleas).

A much more dangerous flatworm is *Echinococcus multilocularis*, which is typically found in foxes, coyotes and wolves. The eggs are passed in the feces and infect rodents, and, when dogs eat the rodents, the dogs can be infected by thousands of adult tapeworms. While the parasites don't cause many problems in dogs, this is considered the most lethal worm infection that people can get. Take appropriate precautions if you live in an area in which these tapeworms are found. Do not use mulch that may contain feces of dogs, cats or wildlife, and

discourage your pets from hunting wildlife. Treat these tapeworm infections aggressively in pets, because if humans get infected, approximately half die.

HEARTWORMS

Heartworm disease is caused by the parasite *Dirofilaria immitis* and is seen in dogs around the world. A member of the roundworm group, it is spread between dogs by the bite of an infected mosquito. The mosquito injects infective larvae into the dog's skin with its bite, and these larvae develop under the skin for a period of time before making their way to the heart. There they develop into adults, which grow and create blockages of the heart, lungs and major blood vessels there. They also start producing offspring (microfilariae)

A dog tapeworm proglottid (body segment).

The dog tapeworm *Taenia pisiformis*.

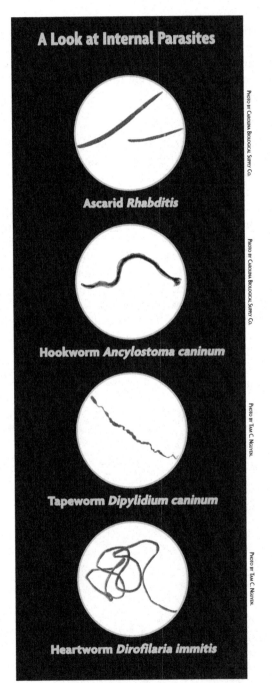

A Look at Internal Parasites

Ascarid *Rhabditis*

PHOTO BY CAROLINA BIOLOGICAL SUPPLY CO.

Hookworm *Ancylostoma caninum*

PHOTO BY CAROLINA BIOLOGICAL SUPPLY CO.

Tapeworm *Dipylidium caninum*

PHOTO BY TAM C. NGUYEN.

Heartworm *Dirofilaria immitis*

PHOTO BY TAM C. NGUYEN.

and these microfilariae circulate in the bloodstream, waiting to hitch a ride when the next mosquito bites. Once in the mosquito, the microfilariae develop into infective larvae and the entire process is repeated.

When dogs get infected with heartworm, over time they tend to develop symptoms associated with heart disease, such as coughing, exercise intolerance and potentially many other manifestations. Diagnosis is confirmed by either seeing the microfilariae themselves in blood samples or using immunologic tests (antigen testing) to identify the presence of adult heartworms. Since antigen tests measure the presence of adult heartworms and microfilarial tests measure offspring produced by adults, neither is positive until six to seven months after the initial infection. However, the beginning of damage can occur by fifth-stage larvae as early as three months after infection. Thus it is possible for dogs to be harboring problem-causing larvae for up to three months before either type of test would identify an infection.

The good news is that there are great protocols available for preventing heartworm in dogs. Testing is critical in the process, and it is important to understand the benefits as well as the limitations of such testing. All dogs six months of age or older that have not been on continuous heartworm-preventive medication should be

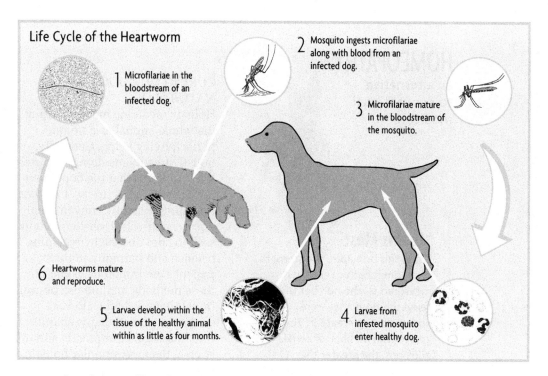

Life Cycle of the Heartworm

1 Microfilariae in the bloodstream of an infected dog.

2 Mosquito ingests microfilariae along with blood from an infected dog.

3 Microfilariae mature in the bloodstream of the mosquito.

6 Heartworms mature and reproduce.

5 Larvae develop within the tissue of the healthy animal within as little as four months.

4 Larvae from infested mosquito enter healthy dog.

screened with microfilarial or antigen tests. For dogs receiving preventive medication, periodic antigen testing helps assess the effectiveness of the preventives. The American Heartworm Society guidelines suggest that annual retesting may not be necessary when owners have absolutely provided continuous heartworm prevention. Retesting on a two- to three-year interval may be sufficient in these cases. However, your veterinarian will likely have specific guidelines under which heartworm preventives will be prescribed, and many prefer to err on the side of safety and retest annually.

It is indeed fortunate that heartworm is relatively easy to prevent, because treatments can be as life-threatening as the disease itself. Treatment requires a two-step process that kills the adult heartworms first and then the microfilariae. Prevention is obviously preferable; this involves a once-monthly oral or topical treatment. The most common oral preventives include ivermectin (not suitable for some breeds), moxidectin and milbemycin oxime; the once-a-month topical drug selamectin provides heartworm protection in addition to flea, some types of tick and other parasite controls.

HOMEOPATHY:
an alternative
to conventional
medicine

"Less is Most"

Using this principle, the strength of a homeopathic remedy is measured by the number of serial dilutions that were undertaken to create it. The greater the number of serial dilutions, the greater the strength of the homeopathic remedy. The potency of a remedy that has been made by making a dilution of 1 part in 100 parts (or 1/100) is 1c or 1cH. If this remedy is subjected to a series of further dilutions, each one being 1/100, a more dilute and stronger remedy is produced. If the remedy is diluted in this way six times, it is called 6c or 6cH. A dilution of 6c is 1 part in 1,000,000,000,000. In general, higher potencies in more frequent doses are better for acute symptoms and lower potencies in more infrequent doses are more useful for chronic, long-standing problems.

CURING OUR DOGS NATURALLY

Holistic medicine means treating the whole animal as a unique, perfect, living being. Generally, holistic treatments do not suppress the symptoms that the body naturally produces, as do most medications prescribed by conventional doctors and vets. Holistic methods seek to cure disease by regaining balance and harmony in the patient's environment. Some of these methods include use of nutritional therapy, herbs, flower essences, aromatherapy, acupuncture, massage, chiropractic and, of course, the most popular holistic approach, homeopathy.

Homeopathy is a theory or system of treating illness with small doses of substances which, if administered in larger quantities, would produce the symptoms that the patient already has. This approach is often described as "like cures like." Although modern veterinary medicine is geared toward the "quick fix," homeopathy relies on the belief that, given the time, the body is able to heal itself and return to its natural, healthy state.

Choosing a remedy to cure a problem in our dogs is the difficult part of homeopathy. Consult with your vet for a professional diagnosis of your dog's symptoms. Often these symptoms require immediate conventional care. If your vet is willing and knowledgeable, you may attempt a homeopathic remedy. Be aware that cortisone prevents homeopathic remedies from working. There are hundreds of possibilities and combinations to cure many problems in dogs, from basic physical problems such as excessive shedding, fleas or other parasites, unattractive doggy odor, bad breath, upset tummy, obesity, dry, oily or dull coat, diarrhea, ear problems or eye discharge (including tears and dry or mucousy matter), to behavioral abnormalities such as fear of loud noises, habitual licking, poor appetite, excessive barking and various phobias. From alumina to zincum metallicum, the remedies span the planet and the imagination…from flowers and weeds to chemicals, insect droppings, diesel smoke and volcanic ash.

Using "Like to Treat Like"

Unlike conventional medicines that suppress symptoms, homeopathic remedies treat illnesses with small doses of substances that, if administered in larger quantities, would produce the symptoms that the patient already has. While the same homeopathic remedy can be used to treat different symptoms in different dogs, here are some interesting remedies and their uses.

Apis Mellifica
(made from honey bee venom) can be used for allergies or to reduce swelling that occurs in acutely infected kidneys.

Diesel Smoke
can be used to help control travel sickness.

Calcarea Fluorica
(made from calcium fluoride, which helps harden bone structure) can be useful in treating hard lumps in tissues.

Natrum Muriaticum
(made from common salt, sodium chloride) is useful in treating thin, thirsty dogs.

Nitricum Acidum
(made from nitric acid) is used for symptoms you would expect to see from contact with acids, such as lesions, especially where the skin joins the linings of body orifices or openings such as the lips and nostrils.

Symphytum
(made from the herb Knitbone, *Symphytum officianale*) is used to encourage bones to heal.

Urtica Urens
(made from the common stinging nettle) is used in treating painful, irritating rashes.

For the many happy years your Min Pin has given you, providing extra care for him in his senior years is a small price to pay.

MINIATURE PINSCHER

The term *old* is a qualitative term. For dogs, as well as their masters, old is relative. Certainly we can all distinguish between a puppy Miniature Pinscher and an adult Miniature Pinscher—there are the obvious physical traits, such as size, appearance and facial expressions, as well as personality traits. Puppies and young dogs like to play with children. Children's natural exuberance is a good match for the seemingly endless energy of young dogs. They like to run, jump, chase and retrieve. When dogs grow older and cease their interaction with children, they are often thought of as being too old to play with the kids. On the other hand, if a Miniature Pinscher is only exposed to people with quieter lifestyles, his life will normally be less active and the decrease in his activity level as he ages will not be as obvious.

If people live to be 100 years old, dogs live to be 20 years old. While this may sound like a good rule of thumb, it is very inaccurate. When trying to compare dog years to human years, you cannot make a generalization about all dogs. You can make the generalization that 12 to 14 years is a good lifespan for a Miniature Pinscher; it is generally a healthy and long-lived breed. The Min Pin is considered mature by three years of age, but can reproduce even earlier. So it's more accurate to compare the first three years of a dog's life to seven times that of comparable humans. That means a 3-year-old dog is like a 21-year-old human. As the curve of comparison shows, though, there is no hard and fast rule for comparing dog and human ages. The comparison is made even more difficult, for not all humans age at the same rate...and human females live longer than human males.

WHAT TO LOOK FOR IN SENIORS

Most veterinarians and behaviorists use the seven-year mark as the time to consider a dog a *senior*. This term does not imply that the dog is geriatric and has begun to fail in mind and body. Aging is essentially a slowing process. Humans readily admit that they feel a difference in their activity level from age 20 to 30, and then from 30 to 40, etc. By treating the seven-year-old dog as a senior, owners are able to implement certain therapeutic and preventative medical strategies with the help of their veterinarians.

A senior-care program should include at least two veterinary visits per year and screening sessions to determine the dog's health status, as well as nutritional counseling. Veterinarians determine the senior dog's health status through a blood smear for a complete blood count, serum chemistry profile with electrolytes, urinalysis, blood pressure check, electrocardiogram, ocular tonometry (pressure on the eyeball) and dental prophylaxis.

Such an extensive program for senior dogs is well advised before owners start to see the obvious physical signs of aging, such as slower and inhibited movement, graying, increased sleep/nap periods and disinterest in play and other activity. This preventative program promises a longer, healthier life for the aging dog. Among the physical problems common in aging dogs are the loss of sight and hearing, arthritis, kidney and liver failure, diabetes mellitus, heart disease and Cushing's disease (a hormonal disease).

In addition to the physical manifestations discussed, there

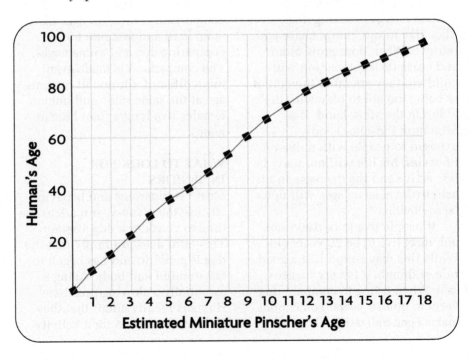

CDS: COGNITIVE DYSFUNCTION SYNDROME
"Old-Dog Syndrome"

There are many ways for you to evaluate old-dog syndrome. Veterinarians have defined CDS (cognitive dysfunction syndrome) as the gradual deterioration of cognitive abilities. These are indicated by changes in the dog's behavior. When a dog changes his routine response, and maladies have been eliminated as the cause of these behavioral changes, then CDS is the usual diagnosis.

More than half the dogs over eight years old suffer from some form of CDS. The older the dog, the more chance he has of suffering from CDS. In humans, doctors often dismiss the CDS behavioral changes as part of "winding down."

There are four major signs of CDS: frequent potty accidents inside the home, sleeping much more or much less than normal, acting confused and failing to respond to social stimuli.

SYMPTOMS OF CDS

FREQUENT POTTY ACCIDENTS
- *Urinates in the house.*
- *Defecates in the house.*
- *Doesn't signal that he wants to go out.*

SLEEP PATTERNS
- *Moves much more slowly.*
- *Sleeps more than normal during the day.*
- *Sleeps less during the night.*

CONFUSION
- *Goes outside and just stands there.*
- *Appears confused with a faraway look in his eyes.*
- *Hides more often.*
- *Doesn't recognize friends.*
- *Doesn't come when called.*
- *Walks around listlessly and without a destination.*

FAILURE TO RESPOND TO SOCIAL STIMULI
- *Comes to people less frequently, whether called or not.*
- *Doesn't tolerate petting for more than a short time.*
- *Doesn't come to the door when you return home.*

are some behavioral changes and problems related to aging dogs. Dogs suffering from hearing or vision loss, dental discomfort or arthritis can become aggressive. Likewise, the near-deaf and/or blind dog may be startled more easily and react in an unexpectedly aggressive manner. Seniors suffering from senility can become more impatient and irritable. Housesoiling accidents are associated with loss of mobility, kidney problems and loss of sphincter control as well as plaque accumulation, physiological brain changes and reactions to medications. Older dogs, just like young puppies, can suffer from separation anxiety, which can lead to excessive barking, whining, housesoiling and destructive behavior. Seniors may become fearful of everyday sounds, such as vacuum cleaners, heaters, thunder and passing traffic. Some dogs have difficulty sleeping, due to discomfort, the need for frequent toilet visits and the like.

Owners should avoid spoiling the older dog with too many treats. Obesity is a common problem in older dogs and subtracts years from their lives. Keep the senior dog as trim as possible since excess weight puts additional stress on the body's vital organs. Some breeders recommend supplementing the diet with foods high in fiber and lower in calories. Adding fresh vegeta-bles and marrow broth to the senior's diet makes a tasty, low-calorie, low-fat supplement. Vets also offer specialty diets for senior dogs that are worth exploring.

Your dog, as he nears his twilight years, needs his owner's patience and good care more than ever. Never punish an older dog for an accident or abnormal behavior. For all the years of love, protection and companionship that your dog has provided, he

NOTICING THE SYMPTOMS
The symptoms listed below are symptoms that gradually appear and become more noticeable. They are not life-threatening; however, the symptoms below are to be taken very seriously and warrant a discussion with your veterinarian:
• Your dog cries and whimpers when he moves, and he stops running completely.
• Convulsions start or become more serious and frequent. The usual convulsion (spasm) is when the dog stiffens and starts to tremble, being unable or unwilling to move. The seizure usually lasts for 5 to 30 minutes.
• Your dog drinks more water and urinates more frequently. Wetting and bowel accidents take place indoors without warning.
• Vomiting becomes more and more frequent.

CONSISTENCY COUNTS

Puppies and older dogs are very similar in their need for consistency in their lives. Older pets may experience hearing and vision loss, or may just be more easily confused by changes in their homes. Try to keep things consistent for the senior dog. For example, doors that are always open or closed should remain so. Most importantly, don't dismiss a pet just because he's getting old; most senior dogs remain active and important parts of their owners' lives.

deserves special attention and courtesies. The older dog may need to relieve himself at 3 a.m. because he can no longer hold it for eight hours. Older dogs may not be able to remain crated for more than two or three hours. It may be time to give up a sofa or chair to your old friend. Although he may not seem as enthusiastic about your attention and petting, he does appreciate the considerations you offer as he gets older.

Your Miniature Pinscher does not understand why his world is slowing down. Owners must make their dogs' transition into the golden years as pleasant and rewarding as possible.

WHAT TO DO
WHEN THE TIME COMES

You are never fully prepared to make a rational decision about putting your dog to sleep. It is very obvious that you love your Miniature Pinscher or you would not be reading this book. Putting a loved dog to sleep is extremely difficult. It is a decision that must be made with your veterinarian. You are usually forced to make the decision when your dog experiences one or more life-threatening symptoms, requiring you to seek veterinary help.

If the prognosis of the malady indicates the end is near and your beloved pet will only suffer more and experience no enjoyment for the balance of his life, then euthanasia is the right choice.

WHAT IS EUTHANASIA?

Euthanasia derives from the Greek, meaning *good death*. In other words, it means the planned, painless killing of a dog suffering from a painful, incurable condition, or who is so aged that

Seniors tend to sleep away much of their days. Be considerate of his needs and provide your senior Min Pin with comfortable warm places to sleep.

Pet cemeteries usually have areas in which to accommodate urns that contain dogs' ashes.

he cannot walk, see, eat or control his excretory functions.

Euthanasia is usually accomplished by injection with an overdose of an anesthesia or barbiturate. Aside from the prick of the needle, the experience is usually painless.

MAKING THE DECISION

The decision to euthanize your dog is never easy. The days during which the dog becomes ill and the end occurs can be unusually stressful for you. If this is your first experience with the death of a loved one, you may need the comfort dictated by your religious beliefs. If you are the head of the family and have children, you should have involved them in the decision of putting your Miniature Pinscher to sleep. Usually your dog can be maintained on drugs for a few days at the vet's clinic in order to give you ample time to make a decision. During this time, talking with members of your family or even people who have lived through this same experi-

ence can ease the burden of your inevitable decision.

THE FINAL RESTING PLACE

Dogs can have some of the same privileges as humans. Your beloved dog can be buried in a pet cemetery, which is generally expensive, or, if he has died at home, can be buried in your yard in a place suitably marked with a stone or a newly planted tree or bush. Alternatively, dogs can be cremated individually and the ashes returned to you. A less expensive option is mass cremation, although, of course, the ashes of your individual dog cannot then be returned. Vets can usually arrange the cremation on your behalf or help you locate a pet cemetery. The cost of these options should always be discussed frankly and openly with your veterinarian.

GETTING ANOTHER DOG?

The grief of losing your beloved dog will be as lasting as the grief of losing a human friend or relative. In most cases, if your dog died of old age (if there is such a thing), he had slowed down considerably. Do you want a new Miniature Pinscher puppy to replace him? Or are you better off finding a more mature Miniature Pinscher, say two to three years of age, which will usually be house-trained and will have an already developed personality. In this case, you can find out if you like each other after a few hours of being together.

The decision is, of course, your own. Do you want another Min Pin or perhaps a different breed so as to avoid comparison with your beloved friend? Most people usually stay with the same breed because they know (and love) the characteristics of that breed. Then, too, they often know people who have the same breed and perhaps they are lucky enough that a breeder they know and respect expects a litter soon.

COPING WITH LOSS

When your dog dies, you may be as upset as when a human companion passes away. You are losing your protector, your baby, your confidante and your best friend. Many people experience not only grief but also feelings of guilt and doubt as to whether they did all that they could for their pet. Allow yourself to grieve and mourn, and seek help from friends and support groups. You may also wish to consult books and websites that deal with this topic.

There are cemeteries for deceased pets. Consult your veterinarian to help you find one in your area.

MINIATURE PINSCHER

When you purchase your Miniature Pinscher, you will make it clear to the breeder whether you want one just as a lovable companion and pet, or if you hope to be buying a Min Pin with show prospects. No reputable breeder will sell you a young puppy and tell you that it is *definitely* of show quality, for so much can go wrong during the early months of a puppy's development. If you plan to show, what you will hopefully have acquired is a puppy with "show potential."

To the novice, exhibiting a Miniature Pinscher in the show ring may look easy, but it takes a lot of hard work and devotion to do top winning at a show such as the prestigious Westminster Kennel Club dog show, not to mention a little luck, too!

The first concept that the canine novice learns when watching a dog show is that each dog first competes against members of his own breed. Once the judge has selected the best member of each breed (Best of Breed), provided that the show is judged on a Group system, that chosen dog will compete with other dogs in his group (which is the Toy Group for

the Min Pin). Finally, the dogs chosen first in each group will compete for Best in Show.

The second concept that you must understand is that the dogs are not actually compared against one another. The judge compares each dog against his breed standard, the written description of the ideal specimen that is approved by the American Kennel Club (AKC). While some early breed standards were indeed based on specific dogs that were famous or popular, many dedicated enthusiasts say that a perfect specimen, as described in the standard, has never walked into a show ring, has never been bred and, to the woe of dog breeders around the globe, does not exist. Breeders attempt to get as close to this ideal as possible with every litter, but theoretically the "perfect" dog is so elusive that it is impossible. (And if the "perfect" dog were born, breeders and judges would never agree that it was indeed "perfect.")

If you are interested in exploring the world of dog showing, your best bet is to join your local breed club or the national parent club, which is the Miniature Pinscher

Club of America (www.minpin.org). These clubs often host both regional and national specialties, shows only for Miniature Pinschers, which can include conformation as well as obedience and agility trials. Even if you have no intention of competing with your Min Pin, a specialty is like a festival for lovers of the breed who congregate to share their favorite topic: the Miniature Pinscher! Clubs also send out newsletters, and some organize training days and seminars in order that people may learn more about their chosen breed. To locate the breed club closest to you, contact the American Kennel Club, which furnishes the rules and regulations for all of these events plus general dog registration and other basic requirements of dog ownership.

The American Kennel Club offers three kinds of conformation shows: an all-breed show (for all AKC-recognized breeds), a specialty show (for one breed only, usually sponsored by the parent club) and a Group show (for all breeds in the group).

For a dog to become an AKC champion of record, the dog must accumulate 15 points at the shows from at least three different judges, including two "majors." A "major" is defined as a three-, four- or five-point win, and the number of points per win is determined by the number of dogs entered in the show on that day. Depending on

the breed, the number of points that are awarded varies. In a breed as popular as the Miniature Pinscher, more dogs are needed to rack up the points. At any dog show, only one dog and one bitch of each breed can win points.

Dog showing does not offer "co-ed" classes. Dogs and bitches never compete against each other in the classes. Non-champion dogs are called "class dogs" because they compete in one of five classes. Dogs are entered in a particular class depending on age and previous show wins. To begin, there is the Puppy Class (for 6- to 9-month-olds and for 9- to 12-month-olds); this class is followed by the Novice Class (for dogs that have not won any first prizes except in the Puppy Class or three first prizes in the Novice Class and have not accumulated any points toward their champion title); the Bred-by-Exhibitor Class (for dogs handled

CLUB CONTACTS

You can get information about dog shows from the national kennel clubs:

American Kennel Club
5580 Centerview Dr.
Raleigh, NC 27606-3390
www.akc.org

United Kennel Club
100 E. Kilgore Road
Kalamazoo, MI 49002
www.ukcdogs.com

Fédération Cynologique Internationale
14, rue Leopold II
B-6530 Thuin, Belgium
www.fci.be

The Kennel Club
1-5 Clarges St., Piccadilly
London W1Y 8AB, UK
www.the-kennel-club.org.uk

by their breeders or by one of the breeder's immediate family); the American-bred Class (for dogs bred in the US); and the Open Class (for any dog that is not a champion).

The judge at the show begins judging the Puppy Class, first dogs and then bitches, and proceeds through the classes. The judge places his winners first through fourth in each class. In the Winners Class, the first-place winners of each class compete with one another to determine Winners Dog and Winners Bitch. The judge also places a Reserve Winners Dog and Reserve Winners Bitch, which could be awarded the points in the case of a disqualification. The Winners Dog and Winners Bitch, the two that are awarded the points for the breed, then compete with any champions of record entered in the show. The judge reviews the Winners Dog, Winners Bitch and all of the champions (often called "specials") to select his Best of Breed. The Best of Winners is selected between the Winners Dog and Winners Bitch. Were one of these two to be selected Best of Breed, he or she would automatically be named Best of Winners as well. Finally the judge selects his Best of Opposite Sex to the Best of Breed winner.

At a Group show or all-breed show, the Best of Breed winners from each breed then compete against one another for Group One through Group Four. The judge

compares each Best of Breed to his breed standard, and the dog that most closely lives up to the ideal for his breed is selected as Group One. Finally, all seven group winners (from the Toy Group, Sporting Group, Hound Group, etc.) compete for Best in Show.

To find out about dog shows in your area, you can subscribe to the American Kennel Club's monthly magazine, the *American Kennel Gazette* and the accompanying *Events Calendar*. You can also look in your local newspaper for advertisements for dog shows in your area or go on the Internet to the AKC's website, www.akc.org.

If your Min Pin is six months of age or older and registered with the AKC, you can enter him in a dog show where the breed is offered classes. Provided that your dog does not have a disqualifying fault, he can compete. Only unaltered dogs can be entered in a dog show, so if you have spayed or neutered your Miniature Pinscher, your dog cannot compete in conformation shows. The reason for this is simple. Dog shows are the main forum to prove which representatives of a breed are worthy of being bred. Only dogs that have achieved championships— the AKC "seal of approval" for quality in pure-bred dogs—should be bred. Altered dogs, however, can participate in other AKC events such as obedience trials and the Canine Good Citizen® program.

Before you actually step into the ring, you would be well advised to sit back and observe the judge's ring procedure. It is best to stand back and study how the exhibitor in front of you is performing. The judge asks each handler to "stack" the dog, hopefully showing the dog off to his best advantage. The judge will observe the dog from a distance and from different angles, and approach the dog to check his teeth, overall structure, alertness and muscle tone, as well as consider how well the dog "conforms" to the standard. Also important, the judge will have the exhibitor move the dog around the ring in some pattern that he should specify. Finally, the judge will give the dog one last look before moving on to the next exhibitor.

If you are not in the top four in your class at your first show, do not be discouraged. Be patient and consistent, and you may eventually find yourself in a winning line-up. Remember that the winners were once in your shoes and have devoted many hours and much money to earn the placement. If you find that your dog is losing every time and never getting a nod, it may be time to consider a different dog sport or to just enjoy your Min Pin as a pet. Parent clubs offer other events, such as agility, tracking, obedience, instinct tests and more, which may be of interest to the owner of a well-trained Miniature Pinscher.

OBEDIENCE TRIALS

Obedience trials in the US trace back to the early 1930s, when organized obedience training was developed to demonstrate how well dog and owner could work together. The pioneer of obedience trials is Mrs. Helen Whitehouse Walker, a Standard Poodle fancier, who designed a series of exercises after the Associated Sheep, Police Army Dog Society of Great Britain. Since the days of Mrs. Walker, obedience trials have grown by leaps and bounds, and today there are over 2,000 trials held in the US every year, with more than 100,000 dogs competing. Any AKC-registered dog can enter an obedience trial, regardless of conformational disqualifications or neutering.

Obedience trials are divided into three levels of progressive difficulty. At the first level, the Novice, dogs compete for the title Companion Dog (CD); at the intermediate level, the Open, dogs compete for the title Companion

The judge will move down the line of dogs, mentally assessing each one's traits to decide which dog comes closest to the ever-elusive ideal in the breed standard.

their Obedience Trial Champion title. In 1977, the title Obedience Trial Champion (OTCh.) was established by the AKC. To become an OTCh., a dog needs to earn 100 points, which requires three first places in Open B and Utility under three different judges.

The Grand Prix of obedience trials, the AKC National Obedience Invitational gives qualifying Utility Dogs the chance to win the newest and highest title: National Obedience Champion (NOC). Only the top 25 ranked obedience dogs, plus any dog ranked in the top 3 in his breed, are allowed to compete.

Dog Excellent (CDX); and at the advanced level, the Utility, dogs compete for the title Utility Dog (UD). Classes are sub-divided into "A" (for beginners) and "B" (for more experienced handlers). A perfect score at any level is 200, and a dog must score 170 or better to earn a "leg," of which three are needed to earn the title. To earn points, the dog must score more than 50% of the available points in each exercise; the possible points range from 20 to 40.

Once a dog has earned the UD title, he can compete with other proven obedience dogs for the coveted title of Utility Dog Excellent (UDX), which requires that the dog win "legs" in ten shows. Utility Dogs who earn "legs" in Open B and Utility B earn points toward

AGILITY TRIALS

Having had its origins in the UK back in 1977, AKC agility had its official beginning in the US in August 1994, when the first licensed agility trials were held. The AKC allows all registered breeds (including Miscellaneous Class breeds) to participate, providing the dog is 12 months of age or older. Agility is designed so that the handler demonstrates how well the dog can work at his side. The handler directs his dog over an obstacle course that includes jumps as well as tires, the dog walk, weave poles, pipe tunnels, collapsed tunnels, etc. While working his way through the course, the dog must keep one eye and ear on the handler and the rest of his body on the course. The handler gives verbal and hand signals to guide the dog through the course.

The first organization to promote agility trials in the US was the United States Dog Agility Association, Inc. (USDAA), which was established in 1986 and spawned numerous member clubs around the country. Both the AKC and the USDAA offer agility titles.

Agility is great fun for dog and owner with many rewards for everyone involved. Interested owners should join a training club that has obstacles and experienced agility handlers who can introduce you and your dog to the "ropes" (and tires, tunnels, etc.).

TRACKING

Any dog is capable of tracking, using his nose to follow a trail. Tracking tests are exciting and competitive ways to test your Miniature Pinscher's scenting ability. The AKC started tracking tests in 1937, when the first AKC-licensed test took place as part of the Utility level at an obedience trial. Ten years later, in 1947, the AKC offered the first title, Tracking Dog (TD). It was not until 1980 that the AKC added the title Tracking Dog Excellent (TDX), which was followed by the title Versatile Surface Tracking (VST) in 1995. The title Champion Tracker (CT) is awarded to a dog who has earned all three titles.

In the beginning level of tracking, the owner follows the dog through a field on a long lead. To earn the TD title, the dog must follow a track laid by a human 30 to 120 minutes prior. The track is about 500 yards with up to 5 directional changes. The TDX requires that the dog follow a track that is 3 to 5 hours old over a course up to 1,000 yards with up to 7 directional changes. The VST requires that the dog follow a track up to 5 hours old through an urban setting.

TEMPERAMENT PLUS
Although it seems that physical conformation is the only factor considered in the show ring, temperament is also of utmost importance. An aggressive or fearful dog should not be shown, as bad behavior will not be tolerated and may pose a threat to the judge, other exhibitors, you and your dog.

Birth Date

Origin (Breeder's Name)

Breeder's Address

Breeder's Phone

Registration/ID Number

Distinguishing Features
IN CASE OF LOST DOG

Vet's Name

Vet's Address

Vet's Phone

VACCINATION RECORD					
VACCINE	DATES				

CPSIA information can be obtained
at www.ICGtesting.com
Printed in the USA
LVOW02s0045021216
515428LV00002B/8/P